AAX-0391
Griffin

W9-BKJ-964

Women as Leaders and Managers in Higher Education

Edited by
Heather Eggins

The Society for Research into Higher Education
& Open University Press

Published by SRHE and
Open University Press
Celtic Court
22 Ballmoor
Buckingham
MK18 1XW

and
1900 Frost Road, Suite 101
Bristol, PA 19007, USA

First Published 1997

Copyright © Editor and Contributors, 1997

All rights reserved. Except for the quotation of short passages for the purpose of criticism and review, no part of this publication may be reproduced, stored in a retrieval system, or transmitted, in any form or by any means, electronic, mechanical, photocopying, recording or otherwise, without the prior written permission of the publisher or a licence from the Copyright Licensing Agency Limited. Details of such licences (for reprographic reproduction) may be obtained from the Copyright Licensing Agency Ltd of 90 Tottenham Court Road, London, W1P 9HE.

A catalogue record of this book is available from the British Library

ISBN   0 335 19879 1 (pb)   0 335 19880 5 (hb)

Library of Congress Cataloging-in-Publication Data

Women as leaders and managers in higher education / edited by Heather
  Eggins.
        p.   cm.
     Includes bibliographical references and index.
     ISBN 0-335-19879-1 (pb). — ISBN 0-335-19880-5 (hb)
     1. Women college administrators—Great Britain.   2. Women college
administrators—United States.   3. Education, Higher—Great
Britain—Administration.   4. Education, Higher—United
States—Administration.   I. Eggins, Heather.   II. Society for Research
into Higher Education.
LB2341.8.G7W65   1997
378.1'11'082—dc21   96-53332
                                                                                CIP

Typeset by Type Study, Scarborough
Printed in Great Britain by St Edmundsbury Press Ltd, Bury St Edmunds, Suffolk

This book is dedicated to my daughter,
    Rosanne Eggins
and to the memory of my mother,
    Florence Iris Parker

Contents

Contributors

Dame Jocelyn Barrow DBE, now retired, has been Deputy Chairman, Broadcasting Standards Council, and a member of the Economic and Social Committee of the European Community. She is also a Vice-President of the Society for Research into Higher Education.

Jennifer Bone MBE, is Pro-Vice-Chancellor at the University of the West of England, Bristol, Chair of the Research and Development Committee of the Society for Research into Higher Education and past President of Bristol Theological Society.

Helen Brown is Senior Fellow and Head of Personal Development, Office for Public Management, London. Her background is in public policy research and she had several years' experience as an academic at the University of Warwick Business School.

Karen Doyle Walton is Campus Executive Officer, The Pennsylvania State University, Hazleton Campus, Hazleton. She served as a Fulbright Fellow at La Sainte Union College of Higher Education and was a Visiting Scholar at Wolfson College, Cambridge.

Heather Eggins is Director of the Society for Research into Higher Education and was elected as a Fellow Commoner at Lucy Cavendish College, Cambridge.

Elaine El-Khawas is Vice-President for Policy Analysis and Research, American Council on Education, Washington DC, and a Vice-President of the Society for Research into Higher Education.

Ruth Gee is Chief Executive of the Association for Colleges, London and was previously Director of Edge Hill College of Higher Education.

Christine King is Vice-Chancellor of the University of Staffordshire.

Robin Middlehurst is Director of the Quality Enhancement Group of the

Higher Education Quality Council and previously worked at the Institute of Education, University of London.

Janet Powney is Senior Researcher at the Scottish Council for Research in Education, Edinburgh.

Yvonne Sarch is an economist who was headhunted ten years ago by Korn Ferry International to be a headhunter. She specializes in Chairs, Chief Executive and senior management/professional posts, especially in the public and not-for-profit sectors. Yvonne is a partner with Howgate Sable and Partners in the London office.

Andrea Spurling is Secretary General of the National Advisory Council for Careers and Educational Guidance, RSA, London and has extensive research experience as a consultant on issues relating to higher education.

Foreword

A century from now, as historians try to describe the last decades of the twentieth century and the first decades of the twenty-first, the role of women will certainly be among the broad themes they identify. With differences in timing and intensity across the globe, these decades encompass a remarkable, still emerging story of women's expanding place in their societies. A special part of that story focuses on the movement of women into leadership roles, and the presence of sufficient numbers of women leaders that, through their collective presence, they begin to exert an influence on their organizations and the society around them.

Women leaders in higher education, the focus of this book, are a significant subset of such leadership. Women who serve as the leaders of academic institutions confront all the issues that women executives face in any large and complex business organization. They also confront unique issues: first, of helping to educate new generations to a broader understanding of women's roles, and second, of helping to shape women's roles in organizations that have a very traditional and masculine cultural ethos.

The contributions in this book offer welcome support to the awareness that institutional cultures and organizational styles are at the heart of the struggle for equal opportunities. As the authors demonstrate, subtle barriers and organizational rigidities exist in most academic organizations. They offer concrete illustrations of strategies that will help to ensure equal opportunity and expand the place of women in the management ranks of universities; of course, such strategies are also applicable to non-British settings. Taken as a whole, the chapters reinforce the point that numerical progress – counting enrolments, appointments, and such – is misleading. Access also must include equal opportunities to move into positions of power and influence.

Similar themes are found regarding women in higher education in the United States. Progress has been dramatic in numerical terms: the representation of women students has risen since the early 1960s, when one-third of all students were female; today, more than half of all students are female, both at the baccalaureate and postgraduate levels. Women have also made gains as members of academic staff; in the early 1960s, women were 19 per cent of full-time faculty; today, they comprise slightly more than one-third of all full-time faculty.

Yet, there is sharp awareness that women are still underrepresented at the higher levels and in positions of authority. Among doctoral students today, only one-third are women. Among members of academic staff, women are found mostly at the lower levels and are poorly represented among full professors. Among college administrators, most women are employed in lower positions and earn low salaries.

Since 1977 the American Council on Education has sponsored a formal programme to accelerate the advancement of women to leadership positions in higher education. The National Identification Program, recently renamed the National Network for Women Leaders in Higher Education, supports state and local networks that identify, promote, encourage and support women administrators and the institutions they serve. There has been significant progress with this agenda. Today, women hold 16 per cent of chief executive positions in US colleges and universities. A decade ago, women held 10 per cent of these positions; two decades ago, women held 5 per cent of chief executive positions at colleges and universities.

During this period, there has been an evolution of thought and focus in the American debate regarding women's leadership in higher education. The general pattern, echoed in many of the contributions in this book, follows three overlapping phases: first, a focus on the individual, and how women's preparation, training and attitudes can be strengthened; second, an understanding of barriers due to institutional culture and organization; and, third, a perspective that looks broadly to the influence of the entire culture and society.

As the focus shifted to the institution, awareness of the barriers to women's advancement broadened considerably. Implicit, unintended, yet systemic biases received more attention. With respect to the cultural practices surrounding the hiring of academic staff, for example, it became evident that subtle differences in the wording used to describe necessary qualifications or types of experience could raise barriers; wording that, on the surface, did not discriminate by gender often was tied to broader behaviours and patterns of experience to disadvantage women who otherwise were well qualified. With regard to women presidents, the American Council on Education's identification programme was premised on a key insight about implicit cultural biases; it recognized that, often, the barriers to a woman's appointment as a college president were not so much in her abilities and preparation as in the expectations and perceptual blinkers that prevented others from being able to see her capabilities as clues to leadership ability.

A third level of awareness focuses on the cultural context established by the wider society, as evidenced in the themes of several high-level meetings recently held among women college presidents. These meetings were based on an appreciation that cultural signals in society profoundly influence women's lives and opportunities and need to be influenced, in turn, if a better future for women is to be gained. This broadened perspective is likely to gain further ground in the years ahead. Increasingly, it will encompass women leaders of higher education institutions in other countries and women leaders in other sectors of society.

The contributors to this volume are valued participants in this important global effort. Their voices strengthen and provide an important context for the efforts in many nations to enhance equal opportunity and advance women's achievement in higher education.

Elaine El-Khawas

Preface and Acknowledgements

The genesis of this book relates to the period when I served the Society for Research into Higher Education as Chair of the Publications Committee. It became clear to the Committee that a book dealing with women chief executives in higher education would make a useful contribution. The opportunity arose for me to undertake the editing and I decided that a book which combined policy pieces setting the context for women chief executives practising today with case studies based on small research projects undertaken specifically for the book and chapters exploring what could be done to implement change, particularly in terms of good practice, might find an appreciative audience.

Here, then, is the book which has taken much longer in the making than at first envisaged, but its essential tenets remain remarkably true. Indeed the fact that it appears at a period of intense change carries certain advantages, in that the ideas in the book chart possible responses to the constant ebb and flow of thinking. As such the book might well be of interest to a considerably wider audience than those principally concerned with the role of women. We hope to offer worthwhile commentary on the changing times, on shifts in employment patterns, and shifts in the idea of a university, as well as scholarly work on leadership and experiential discussion of management. Our aim, as ever with SRHE books, is to offer general readers a range of ideas and insights which might hold their interest and excite their attention.

The Open University Press agrees to acknowledge that extracts of Chapter 7 were first published in *Against the Tide: Career Paths of Women Leaders in American and British Higher Education*, edited by Karen Doyle Walton (Bloomington, IN, USA: Phi Delta Kappa, 1996).

We are particularly indebted to those who have provided material for the survey chapters. Valuable information was supplied by the Commission on University Career Opportunity. The American Council on Education and its Office of Women have both been most helpful. Allen Barlow of the University of Western Australia, Nepean provided valuable general information on the Australian scene, and Leonie Still, Linley Lord and Nancy Warren of

Edith Cowan University, Perth responded to enquiries most generously. Svava Bjarnason is also to be thanked for the time she spent in library searches to support the editing process. But my thanks must go chiefly to my fellow contributors, who all showed great patience in numerous ways: being willing to update their chapters to take account of recent developments, squeezing time out of hectically busy lives to write for the book and allowing me to pursue them unremittingly until the chapter appeared. Finally, I wish to thank my colleagues and family for their support, Emma Sangster for her particular help in the final preparation of the material for the publisher, and John Skelton of Open University Press for his continuing encouragement.

Heather Eggins

Abbreviations

ACE	American Council on Education
AUT	Association of University Teachers
CBI	Confederation of British Industry
CIB	Centre for International Briefing
CNAA	Council for National Academic Awards
CUCO	Commission on University Career Opportunity
CVCP	Committee of Vice-Chancellors and Principals
DTI	Department of Trade and Industry
EOC	Equal Opportunities Commission
ESRC	Economic and Social Research Council
GATT	General Agreement on Tariffs and Trade
HEQC	Higher Education Quality Council
HERS	Higher Education Resource Service
HRD	Human Resource Development
IAA	Institute for Administrative Advancement
IOD	Institute of Directors
IT	Information Technology
MBA	Master of Business Administration
NATO	North Atlantic Treaty Organisation
NHS	National Health Service
NIP	National Identification Programme
OBE	Officer of the British Empire
OWHE	Office of Women in Higher Education
Oxbridge	Oxford and Cambridge
RSA	Royal Society for the Arts, Manufactures and Commerce
SME	small and medium enterprises
THES	The Times Higher Education Supplement
UMIST	University of Manchester Institute of Science and Technology
UNESCO	United Nations Educational Scientific and Cultural Organisation
WOW culture	the individual supplying the service/product/special knowledge
WTO	World Trade Organization

Part 1

Context

1

Leadership, Women and Higher Education

Robin Middlehurst

Introduction

The aim of this chapter is to extend understanding of leadership within higher education, with a particular focus on women and leadership, in the belief that practice can be enhanced through better understanding of the subject. As Adair (1983) and Bennis (1989) argue, however, developing knowledge and understanding through study and reflection provides only a partial means to improvement. Concrete experience, experimentation, feedback on performance and critical self-awareness are also important components in developing leadership. By extending understanding, I hope to stimulate enthusiasm for gaining experience while also offering a sharper focus for the development of leadership capabilities.

The chapter concentrates on three areas: an overview of twentieth century thinking about leadership, perspectives on women and leadership, and an examination of both leadership and women in the context of higher education. These three topics are interwoven throughout the text.

On leadership

The study of leadership has been undertaken within a number of disciplines, each of which has contributed its own distinctive flavour to the subject. These disciplinary perspectives, from history, philosophy, anthropology, sociology, politics, psychology and organizational behaviour, have helped to produce a rich and complex conceptual image. Leadership is thus as difficult to define in theory as it is elusive to capture in practice, and in both cases the influence of culture and values is strong. In the late twentieth century, within western industrialized nations, an increasingly important cultural value is 'gender' and we may expect the idea of leadership to be subject to its influence.

An historical framework of twentieth century leadership ideas provides a useful entré to the subject (Bensimon *et al.*, 1989; Bryman 1992). These ideas can be loosely grouped into six overlapping schools of thought which will be explored in turn, from trait theories to cognitive perspectives on leadership.

Trait theories

'No amount of learning will make a man a leader unless he has the natural qualities of one' (General Archibald Wavell, *The Times*. 17 February 1941, quoted in Bryman, 1986).

The notion that 'leaders are born not made' has a long history and still retains a strong hold on popular views of leadership. The quotation above illustrates a further common belief that such personality traits are typically exhibited by 'great men'. The special qualities that these individuals are naturally endowed with, it is assumed, enable them to be set apart from others and to exert influence so that others will follow where they lead.

In the early part of the twentieth century, psychological studies of leadership were essentially based on trait theories (Stogdill, 1948). Researchers investigated physical features (such as height, weight, physique, energy level, age); individual abilities (such as intelligence, fluency of speech, knowledge and expertise); and personality characteristics (such as dominance, self-confidence, introversion and extroversion, emotional resilience and control). The outcome of several decades of research proved inconclusive in identifying the essential qualities necessary for leadership. Possession of certain traits, while appearing to be characteristic of successful leaders (e.g., assertiveness, decisiveness, dependability, persistence, creativity) did not guarantee success, nor did the absence of these traits preclude it (Bensimon *et al.*, 1989).

Within higher education, trait theories still have currency. Successful academic leaders have been described in terms of personal attributes, interpersonal abilities and technical management skills (Kaplowitz, 1986). Personal attributes include: courage, humour, judgement, integrity, intelligence, persistence, hard work and vision. Interpersonal abilities cover such areas as being open, building teams, empathy and being compassionate. Technical management skills include an orientation towards the achievement of goals, problem-solving, diagnostic and evaluative skills, the ability to resolve conflicts and to shape the work environment. There is a strong degree of overlap in the qualities described here and those captured in more recent, general studies of leadership (Kouzes and Posner, 1993).

Relating personality traits to leadership potential and performance is an area of research that still continues, and one in which issues of gender are also being examined (McCaulley, 1990). Findings are far from clear-cut, however, since it is difficult to isolate inherited gender traits from those which are socially and culturally determined. It is also clear from 'type' studies of leadership (using the Myers-Briggs Type Indicator), that each personality type can produce leaders and that leader-types vary in different organizational contexts (McCaulley, 1990). To date, the research evidence suggests that male and female managers who hold equivalent positions do not differ in personality, leadership style, motivation or effectiveness (Dobbins and Platz, 1986; Nieva and Gutek, 1980; Powell, 1988; Korabik, 1990).

Behavioural studies

Examining the actions and styles of leaders – what they do and how they do it – forms a second focus of research into leadership, and one which was particularly strong in the middle part of the twentieth century (Bryman, 1986). Following this line of enquiry took leadership research away from an increasingly sterile hunt for a set of definitive 'leadership qualities' towards a wider view that leadership could be made manifest through certain behaviours, and that these behaviours might be learned. The notion that leadership was associated with particular attributes and abilities did not disappear altogether, however, since leadership style is often seen as a manifestation of personality (Stogdill, 1948; Fiedler, 1972). In recent accounts of leadership (Kouzes and Posner, 1987; Kotter, 1990), leaders' actions, styles and characteristics have to some extent been conflated.

A central feature of leadership research in the behavioural tradition has been attention to relationships and interactions between a leader and others (particularly followers) and to task achievement and task structuring by a leader on behalf of followers. Bowers and Seashore (1966), for example, summarized the findings of the influential Ohio and Michigan Leadership Studies into four underlying dimensions:

1. Support: behaviour that enhances the followers' sense of worth.
2. Interaction-facilitation: the building of close, mutually satisfying relationships.
3. Goal emphasis: the stimulation of commitment to the achievement of goals, including high levels of performance.
4. Work facilitation: providing the technical and organizational means for goal accomplishment, that is planning, organization and coordination.

These themes are echoed in other works, for example, Adair's action-centred leadership (1983) in which he describes the leadership role in terms of enabling a working group or groups to accomplish a common task, to function as a high-performing team and to develop as individuals. Blake and Mouton's Managerial Grid (1964; 1991) describes leadership style in terms of task and relationship orientations, while Hersey and Blanchard's Situational Leadership Model (1969; 1977) also has two dimensions of leadership (concern for task and concern for people) on to which four styles are mapped: telling; selling; participating; delegating.

It is in the area of styles and behaviours that the issue of gender differences and leadership has been most keenly addressed (Eagly and Johnson, 1990; Eagly *et al.*, 1992). Numerous studies have argued and illustrated that the socialization of females and males is culturally transmitted, with different role assignments and behaviours considered acceptable for each gender (Adler and Israeli, 1988). Interesting confirmation of these findings in relation to leadership has emerged from the work of Eagly and colleagues which investigated both leadership style and evaluations of leadership effectiveness in organizational and laboratory settings.

Analysis of both experimental and assessment studies produced results indicating that women employed a more interpersonal style of leadership than did men, who were found to be more task-oriented. However, in the real world of organizations, no differences were found by gender in either of these two leadership styles. Differences were found in both the laboratory and the organizational settings, in other styles; for example, women were typically more democratic than men, employing a more participative work style. Male leaders, in contrast, were identified as being more autocratic and directive. To complete this picture, a further interesting finding emerged from the evaluation studies. When leaders chose typically masculine styles (such as being autocratic and non-participative), female leaders were evaluated more negatively than were their male counterparts. Further studies confirm the finding that both men and women are evaluated less favourably when their behaviour is gender incongruent than when it is gender congruent (Schein, 1975), gender-based perceptions being 'a set of beliefs and opinions about masculinity and femininity which includes stereotypes of men and women, and attitudes towards the appropriate roles and behaviours of women and men' (Deaux and Kite, 1987: 97).

These findings illustrate the considerable ambiguities that exist in relation to leadership both in theory and in practice. In theoretical terms, it is difficult to isolate those characteristics typically associated with a leadership role (for example, initiative, competitiveness, dominance) from their cultural and contextual values and, in practical terms, it is difficult to know which style is likely to be effective, given that perceptions of appropriateness colour evaluations of effectiveness. These very real dilemmas are expressed eloquently by Judith Sturnick, President of the University of Maine at Farmington (1986; quoted in Green, 1988: 106):

> [Leadership] is a phantasm of cultural stereotypes, and multiple confusions about what is 'appropriate' and what is 'inappropriate' for a female in terms of the use of power, decision-making authority and permissible manifestations of our spiritual/physical/mental strengths. Our culture is a long way from having worked out these ambiguities; consequently, our lives are awash in these waves of confusion, identity crises and overt hostility from both men and women – forces which are intensified for the woman in a public, visible role.

Contingency theories

A third perspective on leadership emphasizes the importance of situational factors (contingencies) – such as the nature of the task, the type of external environment, or abilities of followers – on the emergence or effectiveness of leadership. The ideas represented here are based on at least three assumptions: a) that different circumstances require different patterns of behaviour (or qualities) for a leader to be effective; b) that a dynamic interaction between leader and context will shape the nature of leadership and c) that context and circumstances place different demands, constraints and choices on leaders (Stewart, 1976; 1982).

Contingency theories have helped to extend and refine leadership ideas, moving the focus away from a search for definitive components of leadership to an analysis of the effect of context on leader style and effectiveness. A contingency approach to leadership has become embedded both in theoretical and practical understandings of the subject. It is widely acknowledged that factors such as the position of a leader in an hierarchy, the functions performed by an organizational unit, the characteristics of the task and the technology used, subordinates' competence and motivation to perform, and the presence or absence of a crisis, all have an effect on styles of leadership and on perceptions of a leader's effectiveness. In higher education, a number of 'contingent factors' are of central importance. For example, the technology of higher education relies on professional expertise while the characteristics of the task, or more appropriately, tasks, of higher education rely on high levels of competence, commitment and flexibility from staff. The organizational structure of higher education institutions is complex; in many cases collegial structures co-exist with bureaucratic hierarchies and each of these is then overlaid by political or cybernetic processes (Birnbaum, 1988). These factors militate against autocratic 'command and control' styles of leadership, instead requiring participative approaches which acknowledge the autonomy of individuals and groups.

Gender is a contingent factor which has only recently been taken into account in studies of leadership. Earlier studies sought to understand leadership by focusing investigation on the person of the leader (looking for signs of leadership) and, since these leaders were almost exclusively of one gender, namely masculine, the notion of gender as an important variable in leadership was not raised. Contingency perspectives have changed this picture, assisted by the impact of the feminist movement on both the social sciences and on the status of women in organizations. The growth in the number of women in leadership positions, at least outside higher education, (Hansard, 1990) has brought the issue of gender differences in leadership styles into sharp relief. And, as the research mentioned above indicated (Eagly *et al.*, 1992), the issue of gender is relevant both to leadership and to 'fellowship' since it is in the reciprocity between these two that dimensions of effectiveness are shaped.

Power and influence theories

The idea of leadership has always been closely associated with the exercise of power, whether viewed in military terms as the power to command, in political terms as the power to govern or in philosophico-religious terms as the power to persuade and effect transformation (see, for example, Adair, 1989). In more recent times, studies of leadership and power have sought to understand leaders' power to motivate, to shape culture and to manage change. Within this research tradition, several themes have been followed including investigations of the sources of power available to leaders; the ways in which power is exercised by leaders; and power relationships between leaders and followers (Bryman, 1986; 1992).

In an early and influential study into the nature of authority, Weber (1947) identified three kinds of authority on which a leader's power might be based: traditional authority (for example, time-honoured practices or established beliefs); rational-legal authority (for example, assigned responsibilities within a system of rules and regulations); and charismatic authority associated with a belief in the exceptional personal qualities or supernatural power of the leader. Since Weber's work, different authors have built on his classification, making distinctions, for example, between formal leadership in which permission to exercise official power is granted to an individual, and informal or emergent leadership whereby the exercise of power is assumed naturally or extended tacitly to an individual by a group, often on the basis of the leader's 'charismatic' personality (Etzioni, 1961).

A widely used classification of power sources is that proposed by French and Raven (1968) which incorporates both informal and formal elements:

1. Leaders can influence followers through their positions because of the legitimacy accorded to them within social or legal systems (legitimate power).
2. Leaders can exert influence through their ability to provide rewards (rewards power).
3. Leaders can exert influence through their ability to threaten punishments (coercive power).
4. Leaders can influence others through their knowledge and expertise (expert power).
5. Leaders can influence others by means of their personalities and the extent to which others like them or identify with them (referent power).

Changes in organizations (Kanter, 1983) and better understanding of the internal working of organizations (Mintzberg, 1973) have enabled researchers to propose additional elements, for example, the mobilization of resources and the control of information flows (House, 1984; 1988). Together, these different classifications illustrate a range of power sources which can be deployed in the exercise of leadership. The important issue for practitioners is which power sources are available to them, how they may be deployed, in what combinations and under what circumstances. By examining only the behaviour of the leader, answers to these questions are not easy to come by.

An alternative perspective, which assumes that power is available both to leaders and to followers, provides further insights by proposing that a transaction or 'social exchange' occurs between leaders and followers. Leaders provide services or resources to a group in exchange for the group's approval and compliance with the leader's demands. These services may include financial rewards, political visibility, social approval, administrative or psychological support. In order to reach or to continue in a position of leadership, leaders must take account of follower expectations and be responsive to their needs. Although leaders may accumulate power on the basis of their personalities, positions or expertise, their power is constrained by followers' expectations (Hollander and Julian, 1969; Hollander, 1985). As Bensimon *et al.* (1989: 10) explain it:

> In essence, the group agrees to collectively reduce its own autonomy and to accept the authority of the leader in exchange for the rewards and benefits (social approval, financial benefits, competitive advantage) the leader can bring to them.

The maintenance of the leader's power and authority rests on his or her continuing ability to fulfil follower expectations. Some authors go further and argue that leaders can increase their own power (by what appears to be ceding power) through empowering their followers (Kanter, 1983; Peters and Austin, 1985; Kouzes and Posner, 1987). In these cases, part of leadership is conceived as facilitating the personal growth or task achievements of individuals and groups, which in turn brings increased loyalty to the leader. Power is an expandable resource which is produced and shared through the interactions of leader and followers.

Feminine qualities are often described in terms of nurturing, sensitivity, listening to and supporting others. These qualities are important for empowerment and for current emphases in organizations on teamwork and participation. In recent work on leadership and women, the theme of empowerment is taken up, both as a means of encouraging women to feel empowered to aspire to leadership roles and through emphasizing the importance of leadership through empowerment of followers (Astin and Leland, 1991). Strategies for empowerment include self-awareness and self-belief, communicating with others on their level, offering positive feedback and visibility and working through consensus and collegiality. These strategies are also important in higher education as they are congruent with some of the dominant values of the academic culture.

Cultural and symbolic theories

Highlighting the importance of values in leadership has been one of the major contributions of cultural and symbolic perspectives. Several roles for leadership are envisaged: leaders can mould, reshape and transform culture in line with organizational objectives. Leadership is thus defined as 'the management of meaning' (Smith and Peterson, 1988) and may be linked to different stages of organizational development: the establishment of a culture in a new unit or organization, the maintenance and reinforcement of culture and values in a thriving operation, the transformation of culture at a time of organizational decline or stagnation or in response to new circumstances. Leadership thus assists in developing common understandings about the nature of reality within and outside the organization and serves to highlight those values that are necessary or consistent with the organization's agenda for action.

The notion of culture contains certain features which are relevant to questions of gender and leadership, as well as to higher education. For example, through a cultural lens, organizations are not viewed as concrete entities, but as a network of interactions and events, invented and enacted according to different images and beliefs about how people behave, how things work, or how successful outcomes can be achieved (Morgan, 1986). The importance of facts, descriptions of events, or cause and effect relationships is not their existence, but their interpretation, so that 'truth' and 'reality' are relative. Over time, participants in organizations develop shared meanings that influence their perceptions and their activities. These shared meanings represent the prevailing values, norms, philosophy, rules and climate of the organization, that is, its culture.

Just as organizations are 'invented', so too may leadership be invented through dominant images and beliefs. Some authors argue that this is indeed the case, suggesting that we engender power and leadership as masculine and that images of expertise, leadership and virtue are concepts that bestow political and economic privilege to masculine qualities at the expense of feminine qualities. These cultural values have several consequences. First, they subordinate women to duties that are regarded as less worthy or significant and which limit women's opportunities to participate in public life. Second, men are regarded as the appropriate rulers, and third, women who rule must pass as men in order to rule effectively. This ensures that women will only be represented in small numbers at the top of organizations and in this way, traditions of social order are maintained.

Support for these arguments comes from several sources. Studies undertaken both in the private sector (Morrison *et al.*, 1987; Peitchinis, 1989) and in academic institutions (Sandler and Hall, 1986; McCaulley, 1990) indicate that women are stereotyped as not having the characteristics to fill decision-making positions and are thus perceived as not promotable to those positions. The characteristics demanded of a person in decision-making positions are regarded, typically, as male (i.e., self-confidence, leadership ability, aggressiveness, forcefulness, competitiveness and analytical ability – Schein, 1973; Hern and Parkin, 1987). More men than women are thus assigned to tasks considered important for their organizations and, in these positions, they can exert influence over individuals' futures as well as on their perceptions of self-worth and motivation (Denton and Zeytinoglu, 1993). Denton and Zeytinoglu, for example, found in their study of staff at a Canadian university, that female academics were much less likely than their male colleagues to feel that they participated in decision-making in the university and that this conveyed powerful messages about their perceived value to the institution.

Although the prevailing reality in organizations is of the dominance of male values in management and leadership practice, there are some signs of change. As was mentioned earlier, changing business imperatives are altering organizational structures (for example, flattening hierarchies and promoting team-working), are changing cultures (for example through quality circles, networking and collaborative arrangement) and are gradually shifting attitudes (as flexibility, interpersonal skills, and participative leadership styles become increasingly important). As women reach senior positions, they are able to demonstrate a mixture of approaches which combine 'masculine' and 'feminine' characteristics to good effect (King, 1993).

Cognitive perspectives on leadership

There are considerable overlaps between cultural and cognitive perspectives on leadership. In the former, the role of leaders in inventing reality for followers is stressed, while in the latter, the importance of followers in inventing leaders is emphasized. Leadership is viewed as a social attribution – 'an explanation used by observers to help them find meanings in unusual occurrences . . . leaders are individuals believed by followers to have caused events' (Bensimon *et al.*, 1989: 49).

This kind of transference occurs towards those in positions of leadership for a number of possible reasons: because of a human need to impose order and control or to seek causes for otherwise inexplicable events; because of the prominence of these individuals and the emblematic nature of their roles; because leaders, through their access to resources, are powerful; or because of the leadership 'myths' that surround what leaders are expected or imagined to be, both by followers and by themselves. These images are extremely powerful since they not only define what is or is not within a class of ideas (in our case, leadership) but also shape judgements of effectiveness.

From the discussion above, it is already clear that cultural myths about leadership are strong. This has implications for the ways in which leaders construe their role, for the chances of success in a leadership role, for the strength of follower expectations of appropriate behaviour and for the ways in which effectiveness is judged. All of these issues can be viewed from the perspective of women and leadership; they also have implications for higher education.

The ways in which leaders construe their role determines how they utilize their time, how they seek to shape their organization or unit and how they interact with others. However, a leader's conception will also be influenced by followers' (and others') expectations. A key task for leaders is likely to be to 'negotiate', through communication and example, a set of shared expectations about leadership, and perhaps also about fellowship. In doing this, it may also be possible to address tacit gender-based assumptions about leadership. However, it is likely that where negative perceptions of female leadership exist, it will take time to alter perceptions. Some studies do indeed reveal shifts in male assessments of the effectiveness of female leaders as men gain experience of working for women (Nieva and Gutek, 1981; Heilman *et al.*, 1989). Others suggest, worryingly, that despite 'objective' external assessments of the effectiveness of leadership behaviours on the part of women principals (and even assessments that these women may be more effective in that role than their male counterparts), subjective assessments by teachers of their principal's effectiveness vary depending on the gender of the teacher and the principal – male teachers evaluating the leadership of a woman principal less favourably than did their female colleagues. Clearly, there is more work to be done in changing perceptions and attitudes towards leaders and leadership if women are to achieve their full potential and organizations are to reap the associated rewards.

An important concept within cognitive theories of leadership is the notion of cognitive complexity. This refers to a range of different capabilities including the ability to differentiate and to integrate large numbers of elements (for example, to differentiate between conflicting views of a university's purposes and to integrate these into a range of current and potential university activities); the ability to adapt to different task and situational demands; and the scale and pattern of what an individual can construe mentally, particularly over time. Researchers are interested in the relationship between cognitive complexity and leadership effectiveness, proposing that the need to plan for longer-term scenarios, the increasing complexity of technology and business operations, the speed of change and the paradoxes and dilemmas of the external environment, require high levels of intellectual ability. Cognitively complex leaders are needed particularly at strategic levels in organizations.

Some of the abilities mentioned above are those which women often display, based on their experience and socialization. These include: flexibility and adaptability, ability to handle multiple demands, sensitivity to different perspectives, an approach to life and work which involves a longer-term view of how to make a difference 'for the greater good' of the family, group, organization or society. In leadership terms, these abilities involve both creating an appropriate working climate and setting inspirational or meaningful goals. In research terms, there is considerable scope to examine 'cognitive complexity' from a gender perspective in order to understand better the impact that mental models have on leadership practice and on the ways in which leaders 'design' their working environment.

On women and leadership

The picture that has been painted above is one of considerable complexity, containing a number of dilemmas for women. First, a central message is that the concept of leadership is strongly embedded in gender stereotypes. The language of leadership has masculine connotations, images of leaders are often male heroes (Great Men) and popular contexts for leadership encompass traditionally masculine scenarios (Church, King, State and Army). Common perceptions of appropriate leadership behaviours also carry stereotypically masculine overtones: of command and control, of autocracy and dominance, of personal power or charisma, decisiveness, initiative and courage.

Second, the result of this embedding is that perceptions of leader appropriateness and leader effectiveness are difficult to disentangle from the stereotypes. In studies which demonstrate no difference in the styles of male and female managers or in their effectiveness as managers, we may conclude that 'objective reality' is different from 'perceived reality' and that, in fact, men and women do not differ as managers/leaders. On the other hand, we may conclude, as some researchers do, that women managers are a highly selected group who do not conform to the typical female stereotype (Korabik, 1990). Because management and leadership have for long been predominantly male enclaves, the picture of the ideal manager is grounded in masculine attributes. This may influence both women's career choices and the selection and promotion decisions made about them by others in such a way as to keep women without the requisite levels of masculinity out of management positions (Korabik and Ayman, 1989). As women proceed in management positions, they may undergo a socialization process whereby they become more like men (i.e., more masculine). In this way, they are able to receive favourable evaluations of effectiveness and to retain their positions. Concepts of leadership remain constant and the general cycle of disadvantage for women in relation to leadership opportunities remains unaltered.

Fortunately, some alternative positions are possible, based both on analyses of research findings in relation to leadership and on a wider view of changes in demography and organizational practices. Within the leadership literature, studies of innovation and change (Kanter, 1983; Peters and Waterman, 1982; Kotter, 1990) demonstrate that different skills are now required of leaders. These include abilities to enthuse and empower others by building ownership and participation in decision-making; to build 'thick informal networks' and coalitions; to be flexible and responsive to customer and client needs; to nurture and develop individuals; to be willing to share information and to operate in an open and transparent manner; to be able to articulate core values and to develop culture through the creation of shared meanings. Traditional masculine concepts of leadership are becoming out-dated since they are too narrowly defined; they may well prove ineffective (objectively) in the organizations of tomorrow.

Changes in concepts of leadership are likely to have been influenced by parallel shifts in the environment and operating context of organizations. New technology is changing the ways in which individuals work, learn and spend their leisure time. The amount and speed of change, combined with increasing economic competition, is promoting, somewhat paradoxically, collaborative ventures, benchmarking, out-sourcing, cross-selling and other networked activities. Many of these are changing approaches and attitudes to work in ways which are more congenial to female abilities and constraints. Educational opportunities and demographic shifts are also having an effect. In the UK, by the year 2001, women are expected to comprise over 50 per cent of the work force; they are also starting their own businesses and are entering critical middle management roles. Womens' styles, both those stereotypically female and those less so, are likely to become less exceptional and ultimately, more valued. We may therefore expect that research on leadership and leadership practice in organizations will gradually change its emphases in order better to understand and utilize the benefits of diversity in relation to organizational 'fitness for purpose'. As Starratt (1993) has argued, in a post-modern world, we need leadership which is grounded in an understanding of the human condition as both feminine *and* masculine.

Bibliography

Adair, J. (1983) *Effective Leadership.* London, Pan.

Adair, J. (1989) *Great Leaders.* Guildford, Talbot Adair Press.

Adler, N. J. and Israeli, D. N. (eds) (1988) *Women in Management Worldwide.* Armonk, NY, M. E. Sharpe.

Astin, H. and Leland, C. (1991) *Women of Influence, Women of Vision.* San Francisco, CA, Jossey-Bass.

Bennis, W. (1989) *On Becoming a Leader.* London, Hutchinson.

Bensimon, E., Neumann, A. and Birnbaum, R. (1989) *Making Sense of Administrative Leadership: The 'L' Word in Higher Education.* Washington, DC, ASHE/ERIC Higher Education Report No. 1.

Birnbaum, R. (1988) *How Colleges Work.* San Francisco, CA, Jossey-Bass.

Blake, R. R. and Mouton, J. S. (1964) *The Managerial Grid.* Houston, TX, Gulf Publishing Co.

Blake, R. R. and Mouton, J. S. (1991) *Leadership Dilemmas: Grid Solutions.* Texas, Scientific Methods Inc.

Blake, R. R., Mouton, J. S. and Williams, M. S. (1981) *The Academic Administrative Grid.* San Francisco, CA, Jossey-Bass.

Bowers, D. G. and Seashore, S. E. (1966) 'Predicting organizational effectiveness with a four-factor theory of leadership'. *Administrative Science Quarterly,* 11, 238–63.

Bryman, A. (1986) *Leadership in Organizations.* London, Routledge and Kegan Paul.

Bryman, A. (1992) *Charisma and Leadership in Organizations.* London, Sage.

Deaux, K. and Kite, M. (1987) 'Gender belief systems: homosexuality and the implicit inversion theory'. *Psychology of Women Quarterly,* 11, 1.

Denton, M. and Zeytinoglu, I. (1993) 'Perceived participation in decision making in a university setting: the impact of gender'. *Industrial and Labour Relations Review,* 46, 2.

Dobbins, G. and Platz, S. (1986) 'Sex differences in leadership: how real are they?'. *Academy of Management Review,* 11, 1.

Eagly, A. and Johnson, B. (1990) 'Involvement and persuasion: types, traditions and the evidence'. *Psychological Bulletin,* 107, 3.

Eagly, A., Makhijani, M. and Klonsky, B. (1992) 'Gender and the evaluation of leaders: a meta-analysis'. *Psychological Bulletin*, 111, 1.

Etzioni, A. (1961) *A Comparative Analysis of Complex Organisations*. New York, Free Press of Glencoe.

Fiedler, F. E. (1972) 'Personality motivational systems, and behaviour of high and low LPC persons'. *Human Relations*, 25, 391–412.

French, J. R. P. Jr and Raven, B. (1968) 'The bases of social power' in D. Cartwright and A. Zander (eds) *Group Dynamics: Research and Theory*, 3rd edn. New York, Harper & Row.

Green, M. F. (ed.) (1988) *Leaders for a New Era*. New York, ACE/Macmillan.

Hansard (1990) *Women at the Top*, report of the Hansard Society Commission. London, Hansard Society.

Heilman, M., Block, C., Martell, R. and Simon, M. (1989) 'Has anything changed? Current characterisations of men, women and managers'. *Journal of Applied Psychology*, 74, 6.

Hern, J. and Parkin, W. (1987) *'Sex' at 'Work': the Power and Paradox of Organisations and Sexuality*. Brighton, Wheatsheaf,.

Hersey, P. and Blanchard, K. H. (1969) *Management of Organizational Behaviour*. Englewood Cliffs, NJ, Prentice-Hall.

Hersey, P. and Blanchard, K. H. (1977) *Management of Organizational Behaviour: Utilizing Human Resources*, 3rd edn. Englewood Cliffs, NJ, Prentice-Hall.

Hirsh, W. and Jackson, C. (1990) *Women into Management: Issues Influencing the Entry of Women into Managerial Jobs*. Brighton, Institute of Manpower Studies.

Hollander, E. P. (1985) 'Leadership and power' in G. Lindzey and E. Aronson (eds) *The Handbook of Social Psychology*, 3rd edn. New York, Random House.

Hollander, E. P. and Julian, J. W. (1969) 'Contemporary trends in the analysis of leadership processes'. *Psychological Bulletin*, 71, 387–97.

House, R. J. (1984) 'Power in organizations; a social psychological perspective', unpublished paper, Faculty of Management, University of Toronto.

House, R. J. (1988) 'Power and personality in complex organizations' in B. M. Staw (ed.) *Research in Organisational Behaviour*, vol. 10. Greenwich, CT, JAI Press, pp. 305–57.

Kanter, R. M. (1983) *The Change Masters*. New York, Simon & Schuster.

Kaplowitz, R. A. (1986) *Selecting College and University Personnel: the Quest and the Question*. Washington, DC, ASHE/ERIC Higher Education Report No. 8.

King, C. E. (1993) 'Through the glass ceiling', *Business Woman of the '90s Magazine*, Winter, 8–18.

Korabik, K. and Ayman, R. (1989) 'Should women managers have to act like men?'. *Journal of Management Development*, 8, 6.

Korabik, K. (1990) 'Androgyny and leadership style', *Journal of Business Ethics*, April/May.

Kotter, J. (1990) *A Force for Change: How Leadership Differs from Management*. New York, Free Press.

Kouzes, J. M. and Posner, B. Z. (1987) *The Leadership Challenge*. San Francisco, CA, Jossey-Bass.

Kouzes, J. M. and Posner, B. Z. (1993) 'Psychometric properties of the leadership practices inventory – updated'. *Educational and Psychology Measurement*, 52, 1.

McCaulley, M. H. (1990) 'The Myers-Briggs type indicators and leadership' in K. E. Clark and M. B. Clark (eds) *Measures of Leadership*. West Orange, NJ, Leadership Library of America.

Mintzberg, H. (1973) *The Nature of Managerial Work*. New York, Harper & Row.

Morgan, G. (1986) *Images of Organization*. London, Sage.

Morrison, A. M., White, R. P., Van Velsor, E. and the Center for Creative Leadership (1987) *Breaking through the Glass Ceiling*. Reading, MA, Addison-Wesley.

Nieva, V. F. and Gutek, B. A. (1980) 'Sex effects on evaluation'. *Academy of Management Review*, 5(2), 267–76.

Nieva, V. F. and Gutek, B. A. (1981) *Women and Work: A Psychological Perspective*. New York, Praeges.

Peters, T. and Austin, A. (1985) *A Passion for Excellence*. London, Fontana/Collins.

Peters, T. and Waterman, R. (1982) *In Search of Excellence: Lessons from America's Best Run Companies*. New York, Harper Row.

Peitchinis, S. G. (1989) *Women at Work: Discrimination and Response*. Toronto, McClelland and Stewart.

Powell, G. N. (1988) *Women and Men in Management*. Beverly Hills, CA, Sage Publications.

Sandler, B. R. and Hall, R. M. (1986) *The Campus Climate Revisited: Chilly for Women Faculty, Administrators and Graduate Students*. Washington, DC, Association of American Colleges, Project on the Status and Education of Women.

Schein, V. E. (1973) 'The relationship between sex role stereotypes and requisite management characteristics', *Journal of Applied Psychology*, 57, 95–100.

Schein, V. E. (1975) 'Relationships between sex role stereotypes, ability and requisite management characteristics among female managers', *Journal of Applied Psychology*, 60(3), 340–44.

Smith, P. B. and Peterson, M. F. (1988) *Leadership, Organisations and Culture*. London, Sage.

Starratt, R. J. (1993) *The Drama of Leadership*. London, Falmer Press.

Stewart, R. (1976) *Contrasts in Management; a Study of the Different Types of Management Jobs, Their Demands and Choices*. Maidenhead, McGraw-Hill.

Stewart, R. (1982) *Choices for the Manager*. Englewood Cliffs, NJ, Prentice-Hall.

Stogdill, R. M. (1948) 'Personal factors associated with leadership: a survey of the literature'. *Journal of Psychology*, 25, 35–71.

Weber, M. (1947) *The Theory of Economic and Social Organization* (tr. A. M. Henderson and T. Parsons). New York, Free Press (first published 1921).

2

Women and the Ethics of Leadership in Higher Education

Jennifer Bone

To write on the combined theme of women, ethics and leadership in higher education from the perspective of experience is to invite challenge and dissent. The risks of entering the debate are evident; the justification for the attempt is the conviction that the more demanding the circumstances, the more important it is that the work of higher education should rest upon firm foundations. Three aspects will be considered: the ethical basis of higher education and its goals, the complexities of institutional leadership, and some ethical issues for the leader in person. For women as leaders, each of these fields of enquiry raises issues which may bear upon the ways in which they fulfil their role and exercise their judgement.

The concept of education, viewed philosophically, carries the sense that it is intrinsically worthwhile, in both its aims and processes. Its practitioners have rested their case for recognition and respect substantially on this basis. For higher education in the UK, the stringent ethical framework provided by Newman's *The Idea of a University* became received wisdom in theory, even if only aspiration in practice. Universities have had confidence in their contribution to the common good and to the fullness of human experience.

The pioneers of higher education for women in the last century were moved not only by a commitment to equality but also by the conviction that their struggle was in pursuit of that which was intrinsically valuable and capable of offering reward and delight in its own terms. It was for this reason, in part, that some of the early protagonists such as Emily Davies insisted that the opportunity of higher education for women should be identical to that of men, rather than equivalent or comparable. In the face of allegations that female participation in higher education would undermine the well-being of the family, render women incapable of being good wives and mothers, place unacceptable pressures on their health, and encourage them selfishly to regard their own interests first, the courage and persistence of the protagonists owed much to the depth and strength of their ethical conviction that women should not be denied admission to what was self-evidently good.

The first participants had a sense of both privilege and opportunity. In the process of serving this purpose Vera Brittain wrote of the first women at Oxford:

> they were learning to use their faculties; to recognise and define their aims; to develop a respect for accurate knowledge which was no longer the monopoly of one sex; and to endure failure and disappointment, if it came, with the consciousness that part of a pioneer's equipment was the refusal to accept defeat.
>
> (Brittain, 1960: 64)

This conviction of the inherent worth of British university education found considerable acceptance beyond its own borders. In 1963, the Robbins Report's articulation of the aims and, by implication therefore, the value of higher education in a context of prospective expansion built on this assumption and remained received wisdom for over 20 years. University staff have seen themselves as the inheritors and guardians of higher education's high purposes and on this have rested their case for public financial support.

Sir Keith Joseph's 1985 Green Paper (DES, 1985) ended all that. Although it was regarded at the time, in the words of one polytechnic director, as 'an extraordinarily thin document in every sense of the word', in retrospect it can be seen as having set a framework which has dominated both the operation of higher education and thinking about its goals for the past decade. It gave a nod in the direction of Robbins, but two sentences sum up the paper's main thrust:

> The Government believes that it is vital for our higher education to contribute more effectively to the improvement of the performance of the economy . . . The future health of higher education – and its funding from public and private sources – depends significantly upon its success in generating the qualified manpower the country needs
>
> (DES, 1985: 3)

Martin Trow (1993) has suggested that the Green Paper and subsequent policy represent a breakdown of trust between government and higher education, and a conviction on the part of the former that the latter's claim for institutional freedom conceals simple self-interest and irrelevant performance masquerading as academic autonomy. Whatever the reason, university and college leadership in the past decade has been dominated by the Green Paper's outlook and the policy consequences which have flowed from it. The pressure upon higher education to be more business-like has appeared to many to threaten its character in forcing its outlook and operation to become increasingly industrialized. To the extent that institutions accept a definition of themselves as businesses, they may expect to be judged by the canons of business success rather than by the criteria of an earlier era.

Ethics and the university

A strong case can be made that a primary task for leadership now is a recovery of concern with the ethical basis of higher education and the reassertion on this foundation of the scope and breadth of its purposes. Two challenges have to be faced: one, the social usefulness of contemporary higher education; the second, what may be termed the epistemological climate. The former is well captured by Marjorie Reeves:

> The school of thought which makes competence in the market place the top priority envisages only half a person. It sees the tool-maker and the user; it seeks the organisation of knowledge for purposes beyond itself; it stresses the connection between 'knowing' and 'doing' – 'doing' seen in terms of social usefulness. All these aspects are vital to the life of individuals and communities today. But they embody only a half-truth about human beings.
>
> (Reeves, 1988: 5)

At their best, universities have endeavoured to cherish the whole person, and it is unease at this loss, actual or potential, as much as any regard for vested interest and privileged circumstances, which concerns the academic community. At its worst, the situation involves the leaders of universities in what one vice-chancellor has called 'a miasma of cant', as they argue the toss with their paymasters on accountability, efficiency and the economical management of resources. The weight of pressure has been formidable and the agenda externally driven. Universities are not self-financing, whether publicly or privately funded, and have to serve the purposes of the wider community. Resentment at the need for public accountability, or resistance to recognizing that vigilance, both internal and external, is the price of the maintenance of the highest standards in academic procedure, is unjustifiable. The real danger is of a shift of concern from substance to the language of public relations. The extent to which institutions, particularly their senior executives, come to believe their own propaganda, thereby failing to apply academic standards of rigour and accuracy when assessing higher education itself, is a threat to the ethical foundations and long-term standing of institutions.

The expansion of higher education has compounded the dilemma. Within the system there has been strong, if not universal, commitment to the extension of educational opportunity, which has enabled more students and a wider catchment (a hope not yet realized) to enjoy the experience and benefits of study at this level. In pursuit of this good, staff have grappled with sustaining the customary mode and style of study with a diminishing unit of resource, and with insufficient recognition that the paymasters find the investment justified only by the 'tool-maker' return. Expansion has also necessarily raised questions of diversity and the provision of a multi-dimensional system which legitimizes variations in provision, pedagogy and academic range. The fundamental issue underlying such diversity, however, is not whether some institutions are research-driven, some vocational and some conventionally residential (and far more diversity can be anticipated), but whether going to university or college offers any wider or different experience than that which any excellent training organization developing sophisticated competence can provide.

In a post-modernist environment, however, it may be epistemology which threatens the universities far more than economically-driven social objectives. If the very notion of the integrity of the academic enterprise is suspect, if consensus on the nature of disciplines has collapsed, and if confidence in the authority of scholarship has been lost, then the idea of the university dissolves. The training enterprise readily fills the vacuum. In practice, notwithstanding the intellectual contortions of attempting to pursue the academic life in post-modernist mode, the practice of higher education continues largely as if the threat did not exist. More of its leaders' time and energy could profitably be spent on elaborating the defence so well encapsulated by Ronald Barnett (1990):

> The emancipatory concept of higher education is value laden. It is founded on a belief in the life of reason; and on the assumption that (whether through words or actions) structured discussion aimed at advancing understanding matters. The loss of absolute foundations of knowledge and values (marked by relativism and post-structuralism) does not mean that anything goes. On the contrary it means that we have to accept personal responsibility for any truth claim or value judgement we espouse.
>
> (Barnett, 1990: 205)

On both these issues, the feminist agenda offers its own challenge, not least to feminists themselves. Although from the perspective of post-modernism, 'feminism' as a construct is itself suspect, the view of conventional academicism as serving to re-enforce hierarchical patriarchy poses for its exponents a difficulty in participation in order to challenge from within. As one put it, 'If we feel that logical thinking, the excitement of research, of exploring the world we live in in a comprehensive and thoughtful way are valid aims, have we just been socialised into our patriarchal society?' (Owen, 1994: 97). The difficulty is not of itself resolved by the belief that a feminist academic approach provides a true integration of theory and practice or by laying exclusive claim to a facilitative interactive (feminist) pedagogy as the ideal teaching mode (unless 'management' is seeking to promote it, when it becomes immediately suspect). The richness, human concern and diversity of approach which women bring to bear in higher education, however characterized, is vital to the health of the system; but it may be endangered rather than enhanced by a retreat into absolutes or the assertion of a fundamentalism which attempts to bypass the painful ambiguities of working in higher education or the compromises inherent in grappling with change.

Where it should be possible to find common cause with the feminist agenda, however, is in the breadth of the relevance of higher education to human experience. If, in current thinking, the operational dominates, and university education is concerned primarily or even solely with an instrumental concept of self within an instrumentalist world-view, the role of contemplation and reason is side-lined and the nature of human exchange constrained. The request for evidence for the 1996 National Committee of Inquiry into Higher Education, chaired by Sir Ron Dearing, implies a social usefulness approach to the question, 'What should be the aims and purposes of higher education for the next 20 years?', by seeking comment on the effect of past or future changes on the numbers entering higher education, changes in their background, and in the economy and society on teaching, scholarship and research. Also included, however, was the question: 'What should higher education seek to contribute to the social, cultural, moral and spiritual life of the nation?' It gave universities the opportunity to cast their net as widely as they wished in preparing their response.

Institutional leadership

The link between the view taken of the underlying purposes of higher education and specific institutional vision is evident. The latter, however, has to translate ideals into specific activities, taking account of external prospects and internal capacities. The task requires more than pragmatism wrapped up as values and unless the vision is congruent with the beliefs, values, hopes and goals shared widely among staff it is unlikely to stand the test of translation into reality. Deep and widespread differences of conviction within an institution, or between institutional leadership and the wider community, are a recipe for dispute and ethical conflict.

Like many professionals, academics are notoriously distrustful of the word 'management'. Handy has argued (1984) that professionals are right to be cautious of the term if it carries with it connotations of industrial and commercial practice. Professional work, for its part, requires an environment of partnership rather than hierarchy. Its essence is the exercise of autonomous judgement, by 'licensed' individuals, not hired hands. The variety of roles exercised by each academic represents constant opportunities for the exercise of 'leadership', both formally and informally. Cooperation within the academic community is therefore seen essentially as a matter of willing participation in the making of policy, which one is then under some obligation to support in implementation. On this basis the executive task may then be 'managed' in the conventional sense of the word, but the authority to do so has been bestowed rather than imposed. In her wide-ranging survey, *Leading Academics*, Robin Middlehurst (1993: 49) quoted Harman: the 'community of scholars concept remains a myth of considerable strength and value in the academic world.' It is, however, highly susceptible to self-interested justification and protectionism, masquerading as necessary autonomy.

There is nothing particularly ethical about poor management. The case has been made for the application of 'soft' management to the academic environment in contrast to the 'hard' management of bottom-line economics, the model advocated in some (external) quarters. Trow (1993: 21) has argued that the greatly strengthened administrative leadership of universities in recent years is a version of soft managerialism, which is 'the best defence of university autonomy and in current circumstances the only defence'. This may be to over-simplify. Somehow, the balance must be struck between respect for colleagues' freedom of action (the ethics of subsidiarity) and the organizational need to manage hard choices and to ensure the maintenance of standards in a context of innovation and rapid and substantial change. Bureaucracy in the true sense of the word is not necessarily a repressive instrument. The maintenance of quality assurance procedures, for example, frequently viewed as an intrusion into the proper territory of individual academic judgement, may be a support to impartial and consistent judgement within an institution, and the best defence against innovation of questionable standards in pursuit of short-term financial gain. The converse obligation is that senior staff should resist the temptation to use such procedures as a form of control which diverts legitimate challenge, to allow them to become layers of process which obscure or weaken the university's aims and organizational objectives.

The circumstances of the public sector place limitations on the relevance of industrial parallels; as Drucker (1992) has put it, the public sector has a combination of bottom lines. Higher education is managed for wider goals than profit and should not be seduced by private sector definitions of effectiveness. But whatever the merits of leading by negotiation or seeking to empower colleagues, the senior executives of universities and colleges cannot shirk responsibility for enabling the institution to manage hard choices. The clash of good with good has to be resolved. The allocation of scarce resources to reflect the institution's declared values (for example in keeping with a commitment to student support) means losers elsewhere. A style of management which attempts to embody concern for colleagues is not to be confused with sloppiness; integrity means not letting the organization get away with less than the best. To say so on occasion is not to be in the business of grinding staff down. Care and the expectation of high standards are both deliverable. As Middlehurst (1993: 162) puts it, 'The ability to see the interaction between hard and soft systems, and to integrate the two so that they provide mutual re-inforcement instead of internal conflict is an important aspect of leadership at senior levels.'

It remains of paramount importance, however, that in exercising leadership and responsibility, university executives maintain a strong commitment to the idea of a university and a clear sense of their institutional goals. Stephen Prickett (1994: 180) has argued that the residual strength of the conviction within the academic community remains its best safeguard: 'the British educational establishment can absorb the idiocies of government planners, pay lip-service to them, and carry on much as before. It is a fine tradition, and we should rightly be proud of it.' If so, it is one on which the university needs to keep a strong grip and nowhere more so than among those of its leaders whose responsibilities put them most at risk of a market-driven managerial style. They need to remember that in the context of higher education, as Prickett puts it:

> To describe students as 'customers' . . . is to beg the question of where in the commercial world one may find customers who are not merely willing to purchase an immaterial commodity, sight unseen, but to give an open-ended pledge that they themselves are willing to be trans-formed as people by their purchase.
>
> (Prickett, 194: 180)

Ethics and leaders

Leaders make evident their own convictions in a number of ways, among them attitudes to colleagues, team-working at a senior level and choices in personal lifestyle. But on the core matter of the leader's own personal ethical standards, expectations appear to apply uniformly across virtually all organizations. Integrity features as the key characteristic in surveys of employee expectation of their leaders. Such integrity is understood as consistency and dependability, moral and intellectual honesty, with beliefs and values in evidence in day-to-day operation; it generates a trust which can be undermined by slowness of response or failure to deliver. Such leaders do not manage for self-interest and do not behave as if the organization (or their particular area of operation) did not exist before their arrival. Fairness, magnanimity, belief in others and commitment are other sought-after qualities. It is commonly suggested that these latter qualities are characteristic of female rather than male leadership and that the former rest their leadership in the personal power of influence and staff confidence, in the interests of caring, nurturing and sharing. By contrast, the latter base their leadership on position power and the right to compel compliance. Thus typified, the female leadership style is, unsurprisingly, viewed as particularly appropriate to the public sector and increasingly sought within business organizations. In any educational context, a collaborative team approach, respect for persons and attention to detail may be expected to pay dividends.

Such gender differentiation has been challenged by John Adair:

> All attempts to generalise about the leadership qualities or abilities that women possess, as opposed to men, upon closer examination seem to collapse like a house of cards. There seems little point in labelling certain attitudes or characteristics – such as compassion, warmth, gentleness and humility – as being 'feminine' and the other qualities as being 'masculine'. For these qualities are to be found in both sexes in different measures or combinations.
>
> (quoted in Syrett and Hogg, 1992)

This view draws strong dissent from some commentators. If the research evidence (much of which is drawn from the business environment) suggests little difference in style and behaviour between men and women, this is viewed as a consequence of women adopting the dominant model of masculine behaviour in order to compete and survive. Either way, the woman academic who claims a qualitatively different level of care and consideration for colleagues and students from her male counterparts travels a dangerous road.

Generalizations of any description in this area are suspect; but if they are to be considered at all, then both sides of the coin must be faced. It is at least arguable that the strengths of female characteristics also have their obverse deficits. Leadership in pressured circumstances of rapid change can take some toll of physical and psychological stamina. The routine work load is sapping, the constant debate can cause battle fatigue. Ambiguity and uncertainty have to be accommodated and the position of chief executive in particular has an inevitable element of loneliness. If women add to this an instinctive but undue concern with detail and an over-heightened individualism, the pressures are increased. Where self-esteem is linked to a seductive sense of being needed, the capacity for the selectivity required to maintain effective performance may be jeopardized. On this basis, the implications of the 'service' ethic which is deeply imbued in many women, merit scrutiny, alongside any attribution of male self-centredness. (Expressed theologically, if crudely, the argument runs that if the sin of man is pride, the sin of woman is to collude through misplaced self-denial.) What seems undeniable is that an even balance of women and men in senior appointments would offer better hope for a human working environment with genuine respect for persons.

Responsibility at a senior level commonly involves women in a minority, or sole, position within the leadership of the institution. The need for a senior management group to work cooperatively in the interests of the organization is evident; the expectation is that all members will adopt a common stance of support for corporate decisions, whether or not the argument privately has been won or lost. On the premise that corporate life is essentially masculine in outlook and style, this is the point at which the minority woman may be regarded as most vulnerable to pressure on the one hand or open to compromise on the other. In a genuinely team context an element of compromise is inevitable for every member; but it is also a context in which personal effectiveness is in inverse ratio to consciousness of gender as an inherent impediment. From this perspective, the business executive who remarked that she had never particularly thought of herself as a woman in business, so she had never let it get in her way, had a head start; lack of self-consciousness as a member of a minority does not constitute *prima facie* evidence of a disposition to buy into or sell out to a male hegemony, but it does assist the capacity to participate to good effect in the debate.

Even so, circumstances of deep disagreement and a resultant sense of isolation are always possible in principle. The ethical long-stop is the recognition of the point at which the compromise is too great and dissent must be signalled publicly through resignation. Persistent subversiveness from within soon reaches the limits of ethically acceptable behaviour. In considering the position, arguments of duty, loyalty, mitigation and the capacity to constrain the unacceptable have to be weighed. As Warren Bennis (1990: 126) has written, 'exit on matters of principle is still a distinctly uncommon response to basic institutional conflict'. In principle, however, the issues are the same for men and women and differences of judgement on a scale to merit resignation may be expected to be rare. Where they arise, personal ethics provide one touchstone for distinguishing matters of style from those of substance.

Much has been written about the importance of senior postholders determining their priorities, delegating effectively, ensuring space for dealing with the unexpected, in short, budgeting their time within sensible if substantial limits and maintaining a sense of poise and order. The difficulty for women, however, is that even if this desirable objective is realized in the context of the job itself, life circumstances in total are still likely to take them in the direction of overload. The pressures on all staff in higher education now are significant. The problem is not exclusive to women and men can likewise be torn by the requirements of the job, the demands of family and the inclination to pursue leisure or cultural interests. The problem is most often at its most acute for mothers however; and in general the wider responsibilities of family care and the domestic support system still fall more heavily on women, the more so if they are of a conscientious disposition. The solution is too often found in working long hours and foregoing leisure.

Only the individual woman can decide whether the style of life adopted by one American senior executive ('I don't cook. I don't do laundry. I don't market. I don't take my children to malls and museums and I don't have close friends' (quoted in Fierman, 1992)) represents for her a worthwhile existence. Some may lean more towards the stance adopted by Pauline Perry (1993: 92), the first woman director of a polytechnic:

> I have always believed that my colleagues should accept me as a totality – the mother of my children, the enthusiastic cook and hostess, as well as the HMI, Polytechnic Director or whatever. In taking with me into one aspect of my life all that I am in the other, I hope thereby each is enriched.

Within higher education, working circumstances for staff which permit wholeness of living ought to be seen as congruent with the system's deepest values, although adopting such a lifestyle is always likely to represent a challenge for women in senior appointments.

Ethics, means and ends

The view that an ethical position is to be adopted because it is organizationally beneficial suggests an approach which is fundamentally misconceived. The direct pursuit of 'ethics' as a means to, or as a secondary, end misses the whole point. The question arises in relation to some of the contemporary literature on business ethics and their organizational benefits. The argument runs 'We believe that ethical leadership is a potential source of competitive advantage . . . it benefits the bottom line . . . ethical leadership is an idea whose time has come.' The difficulty with an idea whose time has come is that it is liable eventually to turn into an idea whose time is past. Ethics cannot be regarded as an optional extra, an additional technique with worthwhile public relations or profitable advantages. On the contrary, ethical leadership may find itself with distinct conflicts in the arenas of public relations and institutional prosperity. At the very least the question is raised of what forms of success represent the highest institutional good.

An alternative view is that the concept of ethics in the context of higher education is nothing more nor less than the search for or commitment to excellence. Inherent in the notion of excellence are ideas of consistency, fulfilment and legitimate reward. From this perspective, it is achieved if every member of staff believes in it, is trusted to provide it, and gives it priority in the circumstances of their own work. In an age of unreason, as Handy defines it, 'quality like truth will count, in the end. No one, and no organisation, can live a lie for long. Hard to define, impossible to legislate for, quality like truth is an attitude of mind.' (Handy 1995: 115). Within the academic community, such an approach may enable realistic and relevant analysis of the relationship of institutional strategy, priorities, operation and style. The pursuit of the best stands surrogate for the concept of the good.

For the individual woman or man, however, it is hard to see that the matter can rest there. Whether in choosing between conflicting good, in the treatment of persons, personal standards of behaviour, priorities in living or readiness to take a long-term view, a leadership role requires ethical judgement to be brought to bear, sometimes in an acute form. For anyone in such a position, the formation of good thinking requires reflection on experience, resolution for oneself of the consequences of failure to sustain values and standards, accommodation of new insights and above all the ability to see the role in its proper and limited perspective.

Bibliography

Badaracco, J. L. Jr and Ellsworth, R. R. (1989) *Leadership and the Quest for Integrity.* Boston, Harvard Business School Press.

Barnett, R. A. (1990) *The Idea of Higher Education.* Buckingham, SRHE/Open University Press.

Bennis, W. (1990) *Why Leaders Can't Lead. The Unconscious Conspiracy Continues.* San Francisco, CA, Jossey-Bass.

Brittain, V. (1960) *The Women at Oxford.* London, George G. Harrap & Co.

Connock, S. and Johns, T. (1995) *Ethical Leadership.* London, Institute of Personnel and Development.

Davies, S., Lubelska, C. and Quinn, J. (eds) (1994) *Changing the Subject: Women in Higher Education.* London, Taylor and Francis.

Department of Education and Science (1985) *The Development of Higher Education into the 1990s*, Cmnd 9524, London, HMSO.

Drucker, P. (1992) 'Leadership is a foul-weather job' in M. Syrett and C. Hogg (eds) *Frontiers of Leadership: An Essential Reader*. Oxford, Blackwell.

Fagenson, E. A. (ed.) (1993) *Women in Management. Trends, Issues, and Challenges in Managerial Diversity*. Volume 4. Newbury Park, Sage Publications.

Fierman, J. (1992) 'Developing women as leaders' in M. Syrett and C. Hogg (eds) *Frontiers of Leadership: An Essential Reader*. Oxford, Blackwell.

Handy, C. (1984) 'Education for management outside business' in S. Goodlad (ed.) *Education for the Professions*. Guildford, SRHE/NFER Nelson.

Handy, C. (1995) *The Age of Unreason*. London, Arrow Books.

Middlehurst, R. (1993) *Leading Academics*. Buckingham, SRHE/Open University Press.

Owen, M. (1994) 'Commonality and difference: Theory and practice' in S. Davies *et al.* (eds) *Changing the Subject: Women in Higher Education*. London, Taylor and Francis.

Perry, P. (1993) 'From HMI to polytechnic director' in J. Ozga (ed.) *Women in Educational Management*. Buckingham, Open University Press.

Prickett, S. (1994) 'Enterprise in higher education: nice work, or ivory tower versus Exchange & Mart?'. *Higher Education Quarterly*, 48, 3.

Reeves, M. (1988) *The Crisis in Higher Education*. Buckingham, SRHE/Open University Press.

Syrett, M. and Hogg, C. (eds) (1992) *Frontiers of Leadership: An Essential Reader*. Oxford, Blackwell.

Trow, M. (1993) 'Managerialism and the Academic Profession: the Case of England', paper presented to a conference on 'The Quality Debate', sponsored by the *Times Higher Educational Supplement*, Milton Keynes.

Usher, R. and Edwards, R. (1994) *Postmodernism and Education*. London, Routledge.

3

Outside Academia: The Changing Job Market and its Influence

Yvonne Sarch

Women who seek careers as leaders and managers within higher education are affected by the realities that face individuals in other spheres. The working environment is changing, and in order to evaluate how one can maximize the opportunities available, the individual needs to be aware of current issues and influences.

General economic conditions and changes

Upward mobility has always been an accepted part of successful working and family life. For those currently aged 18 to 30, things are different. Referred to as 'the anxious generation', they seek other fulfilment – which is just as well because automatically doing better than mother/father is now unlikely. For example, moving from the east side to west side of cities happened when new arrivals became successful citizens. Moving from two to four bedroomed houses, going from one bicycle to two cars have been the material manifestations of upward mobility in the last three generations.

Mobility measurement has been based mainly on the American model and even the USA is showing signs of change. In 1955, 75 of the 100 largest revenue-producing industrial firms were US-based. The present top 100 companies are spread across the USA, Asia, Europe and other countries. Two decades ago, getting an MBA guaranteed a fast track to the top. This expectation has been diminished by the worldwide growth of MBA students (2,000 in 1970; 32,000 currently in USA and UK) and by the organizational acceptance of the MBA as being a basic requirement for the fast-track executive on his or her way upwards.

Tough global competition has had a negative impact on the growth rate of the real standard of living, which had previously doubled every 1.6 generations (CSO, 1995). In the 1990s, most senior managers and professionals are wondering if they can maintain the mortgage, the second house, holidays or even their current status. Social/household statistics for the UK show a fall in real income in 1991, with the current earning generation being half as well off in real terms as their parents at the same age. The enormous roll-on implications for career planning are evident. The key factor in planning higher education and continuous training for success at the top is for the institutions to keep up to date.

Manufacturing bases have moved from the UK, Europe and USA to the Far East and developing countries; with them have gone manufacturing employment opportunities. The impact of automation introduced in the 1960s is still being felt. The Industrial Society and the Royal Society for Arts, Manufactures and Commerce have spent much time and effort promoting the idea of linking thinking and academic excellence, design and concepts with industry and production. This linkage is needed more than ever as business becomes more and more sophisticated, global and customer-driven. The study, *Tomorrow's Company* (RSA, 1995) and the current ongoing RSA research on *The Definition of Work* indicate that the individual has to take responsibility for career thinking. Personal development, income and output will be constantly changing throughout all working lives. At the same time, in an era of larger and more open markets, there can be a wider range of economic opportunities for this generation than were available for their parents and grandparents.

Entertainment, sports, franchises and IT networks are the most visible global developments based on talent and shared dependency. Behind each of these there is a phalanx of professionals (doctors, lawyers, academics, etc.). Globalization has added significant new levels of complexity to decisions, and the successful individuals are those who can cope in such an environment. A common characteristic is often a strong educational background rather than just being a lucky entrepreneur. One can argue that to succeed it is necessary to know the conventional and traditional structures, but a willingness to try unconventional and creative methods is imperative.

Capitalism has arguably moved through three phases since the mid-nineteenth century: 1860–1930; 1930–1970 and 1970–1990. The first phase saw an explosion in the establishment of businesses, the second was characterized by government intervention in the economy, while the third phase has seen increasing globalization and technological change. The current effects of the global changes include better worldwide communication and transportation; more economic interdependences alongside fewer tariffs (GATT and WTO), and volatility due to floating exchange rates. For industries, individuals and institutions, life is more hazardous and faster-moving, with more opportunities and risk-taking possibilities.

Changing skills

The 1995 survey by UMIST, CBI and the Centre for International Briefing covered 80 companies and showed that employers are now looking for *special knowledge* as the number one feature for senior executives (see Figure 3.1).

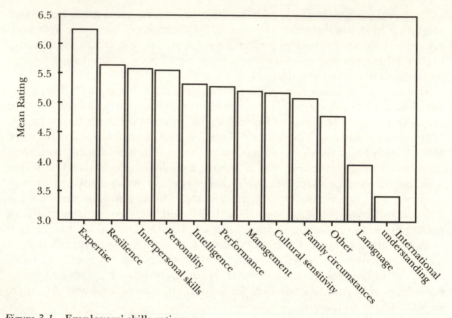

Figure 3.1   Employers' skills rating
Source: UMIST and the Centre for International Briefing Survey, 1995.

This is a reversal, as statistics show that entry to senior management in the last 20 years has shifted away from specialization (marketing) towards general management. In career planning terms, there is a management requirement for special knowledge to be offered by the individual to meet market needs. The importance of higher education offering teaching and training to high and very specialized levels becomes even more acute with the acceleration of the global information highway.

At the present time the average individual career profile has included three employers and eight jobs within a working life. Recent CVs (curricula vitae), however, are already exhibiting changing patterns. More employers or clients are listed, with more roles being fulfilled and more reactions to change being demonstrated. At the same time, over 40 per cent of professionals and senior managers say they have met their own expectations and are happy in their jobs. The prediction is that satisfaction levels will remain around 40 per cent, with the corollary that the 60 per cent could do with help and an increase in awareness of the need for flexibility in their expectations and what they can offer. Unconventional and creative thinking may be as much a part of success as planning and organizational security.

Persistence is the second attribute required by employers in the UMIST/ CBI/CIB survey 1995. The individual must be able to deliver regardless of how that can be achieved. It is a feature which goes beyond structural employment, and covers more entrepreneurial occupations and self-employment as well. The ability to survive, whether it is a major change of location (including country), financial structures or institutional funding is paramount. Not giving up when clients are hard to find, when student numbers are questioned or when personal satisfaction is low, is a strength.

This is the age of imagination and talent. How is this to be identified, encouraged by education and training, and managed?

Following the belief that creativity and talent are winners will produce a more successful career plan. Many colleges and universities have built strong relationships with large firms. Individuals and small firms can benefit too. The two-way flow of information, expertise and short-term contract possibilities should continue to benefit all involved. There is an identifiable increase in the small and medium enterprise (SME) culture (House of Commons, 1994/5). More people are coming out of big organizations to establish their own businesses. Women are predominant in this development. The percentage of MBAs who are self-employed in SME firms has risen from 5 to 40 per cent in 20 years.

In his book, *Crazy Times Call for Crazy Organisations*, Tom Peters' description of the WOW culture, in which the individual supplying the service/product/special knowledge which is required today by the customer (and doing it very well), is borne out statistically. He defines the need to be aware of what talent will create and then find the customer who will buy it, wherever they may be situated globally.

The changing structure of the job market

In just over 100 years, business and institutions have grown from one-man ownership to globally-linked enterprises. Charles Dickens' descriptions (eg, *A Christmas Carol*) were based on the reality of business conditions which lasted until the early part of the twentieth century. The beginning of the twenty-first century may see the return of business centred on the individual, albeit surrounded by high-tech facilities and communication systems in order to deliver the products of creative thinking.

Universities, in some respects still bastions of traditional practices, are showing some signs of adjusting to the new environment. Change in the institutions comes, as ever, at the edges. While contracts have been a fact of life for particular groups for quite some time – for instance, research workers have had short-term contracts for the last 40 years or more – now academic 'tenure for life' has been swept away within the last ten years and there is some evidence of a trend towards the short-term academic lecturing post.

It is, however, in the posts at the top of institutions that modern business trends are most clearly seen. Vice-Chancellors are frequently appointed for five-year periods nowadays and there has been at least one example where the Council wished to appoint for only three years. It is not infrequent for members of the senior management team to be appointed for similar fixed terms. In some cases, usually in the traditional universities, the loss of a senior management post simply means that the individual returns to his or her role as scholar and teaching academic. In other cases, however, usually in the new universities, the loss of a senior management post means the loss of employment within that institution. There have been examples where such a loss has been sudden and unexpected. High pay has meant high risk.

Responses

Implications for the individual career

The most obvious outcomes of recent changes for the individual in terms of her or his career are:

- less job security;
- fewer 'protected' jobs in the public sector, e.g., the NHS, Civil Service, universities;
- fewer internal management roles, e.g. BP reduced staffing/managers by a third in 1991;
- more opportunities for entrepreneurs and risk-takers;
- more contracted-out service possibilities, e.g., consultants in IT for local authorities;
- more opportunities for leadership (transforming a business/profession, such as the 'market' in healthcare; growing a business through franchises; more opportunities in restructured businesses).

Organizations

People are supplying their services through small professional consultancies, or products through SME outlets. This fragmentation is the natural result of introducing ambitious and competitive people into organizations which have changed from vertical hierarchies to much flatter structures with fewer core roles and shorter career ladders than imaginable ten years ago: ambitious people seek other ways to make their mark. Small firms (under 500 employees) have comparative advantages in fast-moving business environments: their relative flexibility allows them to respond rapidly to market demands. Modern communications, Business Park facilities and various enterprise initiatives, both public and private, all assist the setting-up and running of small businesses. Whereas in 1970 most people who left college and university accepted an offer from a large company or industry, in the 1990s graduates have to find openings wherever possible.

People's attitudes to employment are also showing signs of change. More and more academics and executives are showing a reluctance to moving their families regularly. Many large organizations are seen as uncongenial because of their levels of bureaucracy, and many people have either left or started to seek to change the whole structure through individual and group influence.

Fulfilment is sought in different ways. The opportunity to expand knowledge and spread influence is a key factor for those who are ambitious; some achieve this through being a large fish in a small pond, while others are motivated by organizational status. Employers can be caught in a dilemma. Talented (maybe eccentric) people may leave traditional/bureaucratic organizations to make more money and to have more autonomy. Yet such organizations need good people and astute senior managers try not to lose them or, if they do, to replace them as quickly as possible. (Philip Sadler [1993] in *Managing Talent*, discusses many aspects of these dilemmas.)

Within higher education it is sometimes the most imaginative, opportunistic staff who offer to take early retirement, and their loss can have damaging effects. Often the people most affected when key senior people leave are staff at lower levels who have been inspired and motivated by the leadership qualities of that person. This has a knock-on effect on the organization.

In Peters and Waterman's book *In Search of Excellence* (1982) there was the first glimmer of understanding of how inwardly-focused organizations such as universities, with highly competitive key people/leaders, were not achieving maximized results. Tom Peters has confirmed his appraisals of corporate cultures in his more recent books (Peters, 1994; 1995). He sees the *power of the individual* based in the use of highly creative thinking and knowledge for the discerning and paying customer. Externally-focused small organizations or parts of big ones are more effective than internally-focused ones. Competitive cultures which are driven by politics and jealousies are not as effective as those which are clear in their thinking and strategy.

SMEs create more jobs than big firms and are predicted to continue doing so (UMIST and the Centre for International Briefing, 1995). The destructuring and decline of big organizations in the late 1980s and early 1990s have seen people being re-employed without being put on the payroll – making many good people available on a project or advisory basis. The 'small is beautiful' idea has become a self-fulfilling prophecy. Success is going to the small, risk-taking entrepreneurs inside and outside the organization. People (leaders), who found and grow their business, even within the academic world, can expect more job satisfaction and even more income than those maintaining their position on the payroll within traditional structures. The shock of redundancy can be a blessing in disguise for some, who can turn it into an opportunity.

Within the new context people who make things happen are the successful leaders; the powerful individual becomes the supplier, the distributor, banker, consultant, producer, expert or temporary colleague to fulfil the needs of the customer/client. More and more the perception is that value is added more easily from the outside (the unfamiliar) than from the inside (the familiar).

Network organizational structures are likely to become more flexible, dynamic, innovative and competitive. Visionary entrepreneurs frequently do not have the capacity to be good managers and developers of people, and they need to recognize when to hand over. The follow-on and maintenance of a continuing competitive edge needs management and a different kind of leadership. Stephen Covey in *The Seven Habits of Highly Effective People* (1989) expands on this theme.

There are few guaranteed long-term employment prospects left. More and more short-term contracts are available, and many have to initiate their own occupations rather than depend on others for funding or employment. One in ten senior people are in this situation today. Employment through consultancy is the fastest growing trend (Manpower Inc. (USA), 1996). It is a nerve racking mix of marketing and delivery which has uncertainty at all stages. Such changes in working patterns can destabilize personal and family life unless the change is planned for and accepted. Those who aspire to positions of leadership in higher education, as in any other field, need to recognize these realities. Rosabeth Moss Kanter in *The Change Masters* (1983) forecast the tensions between the individual and the group, personal motivations and the environment, and getting things done and being 'nice'.

Success depends on leadership, not just good management or academic input. Even at lower levels, the ability to lead affects organizational performance and individual careers, and the gap between the winners and others is widening. The individual has got to be an able competitor equipped with especially high standards (and qualifications) and the strong desire to win. The ability to continuously learn new approaches, skills, techniques and understanding is aided by strong foundation learning. This is as true within higher education as it is elsewhere – and so is the need for political skills. The nature of change is that it tends to shake up established power structures. This bodes well for the individual as opportunities and risks are there to be taken. The woman who wishes to succeed as leader and manager in higher education needs to develop the capacity to recognize and take advantage of the opportunities that are offered.

Bibliography

Central Statistical Office (CSO) (1995) *Social Trends*, 25. London, HMSO.
Century Business (1992) *How to be Headhunted. How to make yourself the best person for the best job.* London, Century Business.
Covey, S. R. (1989) *The Seven Habits of Highly Effective People.* New York, Simon & Schuster.
House of Commons (1994/5) 821 *Special Report. Trade and Industry Committee Report on Small Business Sector.*
Jones, S. and Sarch, Y. (1992) *How to be Headhunted Across Europe.* London, Macmillan.
Manpower Inc. (USA) (1996) *Annual Company Report.*
Moss Kanter, R. (1983) *The Change Masters.* London, Unwin.
Moss Kanter, R. (1996) *World Class.* New York, Simon & Schuster.
Peters, T. and Waterman, R. H. (1982) *In Search of Excellence.* London, Macmillan.
Peters, T. (1994) *Crazy Times Call for Crazy Organisations.* London, Macmillan.
Royal Society of Arts (1995) 'Tomorrow's Company', *RSA Enquiry.*
Peters, T. (1995) *The Pursuit of WOW.* London, Macmillan.
Sadler, P. (1993) *Managing Talent.* Ashridge, Ashridge Management College.
UMIST and the Centre for International Briefing (1995) *Report on Employer/Employee Expectations.* Farnham Castle.

Part 2

Case Studies

4

Women and Change in Higher Education

Andrea Spurling

Change and no change

Following the dissolution of the binary system in 1992, higher education institutions have been finding their place in a unified but diverse sector, variously buttressed and buffeted by changes in structure and funding policies. Credit accumulation and transfer, new phasing of course delivery, and new modes of teaching and learning within and beyond the institution have been adopted by many. New partnerships have developed in and among universities and colleges of higher education; between them and colleges of further education; and between higher education, further education and employers in the private and public sectors.

Government ministers like to represent this upheaval as the formal democratization of the system – a step towards John Major's 'classless society'. But those educated in long-established academic conventions know higher education as a social organism, not as a design-and-build enterprise. Real democratization needs more than the admission of more kinds of people in more kinds of ways: it demands the restructuring and redistribution of power. The form of higher education may evolve but it is the dominant culture that determines access to institutional power, in higher education as in parliament. The new sector embraces institutions from very different traditions, but history illustrates the tenacity of the academic culture. Its superior social status and the funding it attracts have drawn in even those institutions established to provide alternative technical education and training. Over the years technicians' institutes, technical colleges, colleges of advanced technology and polytechnics have drifted steadily into the university sector.

A profound cultural change will need to take place if the pattern is not to be repeated. It is different kinds of people, not different ideas, that change cultures. More kinds of people are entering higher education but the culture will only change if they stay and move to positions of professional power and influence. This chapter looks at ways in which women can contribute to such a change, and the experience of some who have tried to effect it.

Change and integrity

. . . how to conjure integrity out of pluralism remains higher education's most urgent task at the end of the 20th century. Or, better still, how to redescribe notions of excellence, referenced in the past, in terms of an integrity that is future-directed, and how to redefine a threatening confusion as a more hopeful pluralism.

(Peter Scott, *THES*, 28 August 1992)

Real integrity is multi-dimensional. It comes from integrating differences in a harmonized whole, and from the resonance of the whole with its context. In terms of vigour and growth, pluralism is less of a threat to integrity in higher education than the polarizing dynamics of a contentious culture in which people are either a success or a failure; in or out; one of us or one of them. Such dynamics do not create integrity; they seek to protect cultural purity – and the twentieth century continues to show what a dangerous aim that can be. In the task of 'conjuring integrity out of pluralism' groups that were previously marginalized have their own unique contribution to make. Women have a particular role to play in rectifying the balance of gender in content, in form, and in person.

The revolving door

Although access to higher education for non-standard entrants has improved, there is still a long way to go to remove cultural barriers altogether. Taylor (1992) has shown why it is the routes, not only the points of access, that need attention and monitoring if traditional barriers are to be removed. Changes that broaden access often do little more than that. The more foreign non-standard entrants are to the dominant culture, the sooner they leave, resulting in the last-in-first-out movement of apparently self-selecting groups of students. The origins of such selection actually lie in the undeclared biases of the institutional culture, the enigmatic and implicit nature of which makes them difficult to identify, acknowledge and address.

The result may be a minor disadvantage for people who value academic qualifications primarily as passports to professional training completed elsewhere. More people will gain the experience in higher education necessary for professional status; this will improve the community service record of the institutions at undergraduate level, potentially raising the skills level of the nation's labour force in the process. But the real and visible benefits of this tend to disguise the lost opportunity such a movement represents for the academic profession itself: an increased flow of people through the lower reaches of the institutions does not nourish it in the upper regions. This can only be achieved by appointing and promoting new talent of the best quality; exploring and incorporating new areas of study that coincide with the interests of a changing student body in the process. It is bound to be a reciprocal process, the new talents and areas of work changing the very nature of the quality by which they are assessed.

Quality and gender

A plethora of conferences, consultations, seminars, debates, colloquiums (or colloquia, according to venue) and articles in the professional press examine the dilemma in defining 'quality' for the new higher education sector. A successful result will redefine the academic profession to include people at all professional levels whose lives, interests and ways of working do not fit the established conventions. But *quis custodiet ipsos custodes?* Can the academic profession redefine itself? The position of women in higher education is evidence of its resistance to doing just that.

The formal institutions that control educational opportunity and what constitutes validated knowledge are especially significant in maintaining the double standard that upholds the 'sequestration of experience' in modern social institutions (Giddens, 1992). It has resulted in the overall gender imbalance in favour of masculine experience and criteria in the curriculum, in ways of working, and in staffing. That imbalance actively discriminates against women, but it does not affect women only. Gender is not sex: culturally, masculinity and femininity are not synonymous with maleness and femaleness.

Gender affects the distribution of prestige and therefore also the routes to power. Until very recently academic career progress to senior levels relied almost entirely on research-based work, with the result that opportunities for research, publication and attendance at conferences directly affected the possibility of promotion. Many academic women say they are under pressure to accept a heavier teaching load and more pastoral care than their male colleagues. Teaching is seen to fit in with family life better than research and, whether they intend it or not, women are expected to bear the major responsibility for hands-on family care. But it is not only a question of sex. Men who bear a major domestic/caring role over a long period also have reduced opportunity for the work that supports promotion. Moving into a traditionally feminine area of activity delays academic career progress.

The detrimental effects of gender imbalance do not only affect people with long-term academic ambitions. Undergraduate experience influences the ambitions and expectations of all graduates, male or female, wherever they seek to develop careers. The superior weight given to masculine criteria, thoroughly embedded in the human and intellectual environment of the institutions, exerts as powerful an influence by example and implication as anything explicitly stated. Despite the increasing development of policies for equal opportunities, this influence remains unconscious in many areas of study, unacknowledged and a source of professional sabotage for women in industry and the professions beyond the academy.

One example of embedded masculinity is the extent to which gender discrimination even affects institutional prestige in recreational activities. This may seem a petty issue to observers, but the accumulated effects of relentless discrimination can steadily undermine the confidence and energy of those subject to it. In 1992 the Cambridge [University's] Dancer's Club, which had expanded from 200 to 2,000 members in ten years, was refused recognition by the University's men's sporting blues committee, although the women's committee had accepted ballroom dancing as a sport the previous year. The male committee secretary's comment to the press reverberated with the deep, rich tones of unalloyed prejudice: 'We just decided it simply isn't in the same category as things we regard as sport.'

Working cultures

> . . . can non-traditional students be tolerated only as long as they are too small a minority to risk altering campus culture?
>
> Remember that 'traditional' applies to contemporary British *notions* of a 'normal university education', not necessarily to past or present practice in Britain or abroad. [Italics in the original.]
>
> (Duke, 1992: 62)

University *practice* has increasingly recognized the importance of service to the wider community, certainly in attracting funding. But this has scarcely yet affected the *cultural ideal* of a university: a physically defined space sacred to the exercise of academic freedom; a base for research; a storehouse of authenticated knowledge; and an arena for adolescent rites of passage. The popular perception of the university culture, especially among people who have never been to university themselves, is back-lit by Merchant and Ivory in muted tones of nostalgia and exclusivity. The effect of such perceptions on marketing was the reason many polytechnics gave when they chose to don quasi-medieval regalia on joining the university sector.

It may help to pull in the punters, but what about the workers? The traditional collegiate associations of the culture have made many universities slow to accept their responsibilities as employers. They have preferred to regard those who work in them as junior and senior club members, treated to the benefits and drawbacks of institutional paternalism. Even academics whose own work expands egalitarian theory function in institutions where real equality of opportunity has yet to become established.

Central government has demanded and procured improved management at all levels in higher education. So much, yet so little, has changed. Academics have learned the language and style of managerialism, and people with management experience from industry – a world with problems of gender imbalance at least as great as those in higher education – have been appointed to university posts. What is culturally significant in the long run is how fundamentally such changes can alter the distribution of power.

Cultural annexation

Women's academic careers are a barometer of change in higher education, and their accumulated experience shows that there will have to be a more profound change for real power-sharing to happen. Generations of women have passed through higher education and added to the store of academic knowledge, but their history is of cultural annexation rather than incorporation. The cultural forces that inhibit the full establishment of women's academic interests also inhibit their access to senior management, preventing all but a few from gaining the range of experience and contacts needed by senior policy makers and power-holders anywhere. Most are in insecure, poorly paid, low status posts, where they perform the traditional role of women in every workforce: providing flexibility to the system at the cost of their own professional development.

Women are entering higher education as students in rapidly increasing numbers, many as confident and determined adults. In a briefing paper prepared for the National Commission on Education, Professor A. H. Halsey showed that between 1970 and 1989 there had been a 30 per cent increase in the number of full-time female undergraduates at universities, compared with a 20 per cent increase in the number of males. Over the same period there had been a 758 per cent increase in the proportion of women studying part-time at the then polytechnics and colleges of higher education. Part-time study, especially at undergraduate level, is expensive for students financially and in personal terms (Bourner *et al.*, 1991; Tight, 1991). People who engage in it have to be well focused and tenacious if they are to succeed. As non-traditional students they experience low institutional status at high personal cost, yet these are the people who represent a rich resource for a nation aiming to increase the size and scope of its graduate labour force over a short period.

It is changes of this kind at the boundaries that have brought pressure to bear on the centre of higher education. It has shifted the balance between teaching and research; between undergraduate and graduate students; between public and private funding; and between internal and external focus. It provides the friction heating the debate about academic authority and quality in the academy, and it is here that greater risks will have to be taken if a genuinely new identity is to be forged for the sector.

Women's studies and cultural deviance

Academic authority is consistently retrospective. The backward glance is so instinctive that the evolution of higher education itself is named to perpetuate the features and divisions of earlier forms. Developments have been realized in a language which presents them as deviants of an established norm: non-*collegiate* universities; *extramural* courses; post-*binary* system; non-*standard* entrants; non-*traditional* students. Time drags between change in practice and its acceptance into the culture. Naming development in mincing steps hobbles its cultural progress and maintains a sense of historic divisions.

This reluctance to give developments substance except in terms of what is already established is epitomized by the history of women's studies in Britain. The institutions have balked at granting full academic authority to a subject that focuses unequivocally on what it is rather than what it is not:

> . . . Women's Studies has never attained the recognition here it enjoys in the US or Europe. Figures by the European Women's Studies Network show that the Netherlands has 14 Women's Studies' Chairs, Denmark five. But although Britain is the only European country with a full degree in the subject (at the University of East London) and although courses offered are still increasing, Britain has only one chair, at the University of Ulster.
>
> (Sian Griffiths, *THES*, 4 September 1992)

In identifying itself by gender, women's studies draws attention to the institutional 'sequestration of experience' and implicitly challenges the gender imbalance of other academic studies. It consequently exposes their claims to intellectual objectivity and neutrality as more conventional than real.

At the beginning of 1993 the *Times Higher Educational Supplement* reported that university women's studies courses had received 'a glowing report' from HMI Inspectorate. It also indicated the conditions under which this had been achieved.

> [Courses] are successful in attracting students traditionally excluded from higher education, yet still achieve high standards. . . . [Mary Evans, director of women's studies at the University of Kent] said: 'The rigid compartmentalisation at many universities is threatening women's studies because it means it does not get direct funding . . . [it is] being starved of funds.'. . .
>
> Committed staff are usually based in another subject area which has first call on their services and often over extend themselves rather than let courses fail to run, the [HMI] report adds.
>
> (*THES*, 5 February 1993)

Women's contribution to scholarship

Thorough scholarship provides the chink through which women's studies and feminist theory and critique could gain academic respectability, exert an institutional influence, and contribute to real professional and institutional integrity in the new higher education. Women's new and critical interpretations expand knowledge: studies from a non-masculine viewpoint lead to a broader interpretation and deeper comprehension of validated knowledge.

Such studies also represent added value for the institutions. Women's experience has cash value in a funding system that now actively seeks to promote the importance of good teaching and to reward the scholarship associated with institutional development. This is professional regeneration, not prostitution. Properly supported by the institution, as all new subjects need to be if they are to flourish, women's studies and feminist critique provide bases that encourage women to enter higher education and to develop careers within it. In doing so they broaden the scope of academic enquiry and play a part in redefining it.

First-hand experience

This section is based on individual interviews with women in senior posts in higher education. The interviewees were selected because of their experience as holders of senior office, and for the light they could throw on particular aspects of women's careers in higher education. Each life story was unique, of course, but many of the elements relating to their career histories were common to the experience of women in higher education in Britain and elsewhere.

At the time of the interviews two of the women were in formal dispute with institutions that currently or formerly employed them; three were working in new universities; one worked in a university established during the 1960s on a greenfield site; one in a university combining greenfield and city origins; one in a redbrick university. The institutions were geographically widespread across England and Ireland.

Two of the women were professors (one a pro-vice-chancellor); one was a senior lecturer and one a former dean; one was a dean; and one an academic registrar. They were aged between 38 and 50 when interviewed. All were white; one was not British by birth; most described themselves as coming from middle-class homes. All had been married at some time; four of the six were separated or divorced; one was married and living with her husband; one was a 'telegamous' marriage, having lived for ten years mostly in a different place from her husband in the interests of her career development. Three of the women had two children each, most of them in their teens, and one was the parent of an undergraduate. Two had no children – one voluntarily. One mother of two children had become a lesbian at the age of 40:

> I see this as quite a logical progression from my feminist principles and experiences at work. . . . I would have found it much harder, or even impossible, to have left my husband and become a lesbian had he not moved to a new job over three hours' drive away.

One woman had done her undergraduate degree as a mature student, after working in a non-academic field. Two of the six had specialized in traditional academic subjects, one being the editor of an international academic journal in her subject; the other four had helped to develop women's studies, feminist critique and theory, and social welfare. They had all been involved in the development of equal opportunities policies in their institutions.

The women used the interviews to discuss structural and cultural factors in higher education affecting academic and academic-related careers, curriculum content, teaching and research, institutional organization, leadership in higher education, and aspects of their own professional and personal experience.

Professional women

The women working in traditional universities had had typically different experiences from those in new universities. Mostly this reflected differences in institutional aims and the constitution of the student bodies. They reported similar experiences of institutional gender imbalance, but attributed it to different causes. What the three women in traditional universities attributed to 'academic machismo' was also identified by two in new universities as 'machismo of the business culture'. The sixth was the only one to describe a growing power-base of senior women in her institution (see below).

The interviews necessarily focused on areas of professional frustration. In different ways, as each interview progressed, four of the women increasingly displayed an underlying intensity of managed anger. The extent to which they had learned to use this constructively seemed to reflect the extent of the formal and informal support they had found, personally and institutionally. The more isolated they felt – as individuals in their institutions, geographically, and in their personal lives – the more exhaustion they expressed. One said, 'Exhaustion is inevitable for senior women. What you have to avoid is burn-out.'

Non-academic experience

The remaining two women provided an interesting contrast. They had not had conventional academic careers only. One had been a mature-age undergraduate, after having had children and being in non-academic employment. She had subsequently been actively involved in trade union work as an academic and described the experience as valuable management training: 'I had the confidence to sit back and learn, mostly from men. . . . I was being used, but the trade-off for me was good.'

At the time of the interview she was working in an institution with a strong tradition of service to the local multi-racial community, and catering for a relatively high proportion of adult and part-time students. She described the progress of equal opportunities in her university as 'a steep institutional learning curve'. This was based on widespread and open discussion of the issues in general, and sensitive handling of individual cases including same-sex harassment (of women by women), homophobia and heterosexism. She saw informed institutional confidence as an important benefit of open discussion: 'We're quite tough with students who use sexism or racism as a cop out.'

This confidence was also reflected in a body of female deans in the institution large enough to create a critical mass of women in senior management: 'We're powerful, we're wealthy, and there are a lot of us.'

The sixth woman's academic career path had started as a lecturer in an ancient university but had been disrupted when she followed an early career move by her husband. 'I suddenly discovered what it meant to be *defined* as a wife.' By the age of 30 she found she was 'very busy with short-term academic jobs, but had no career'. She was appointed to an administrative post in the then polytechnic sector (having rejected the recommendation of a university careers adviser that she retrain as an accountant) and immediately became aware of a different form of professional sexism: 'It was assumed that if you were a woman in polytechnic administration you probably did not have a degree.'

The attitudes of her colleagues gave her higher social status as an ex-university lecturer than as a polytechnic administrator, although her temporary academic work had had lower employment status than the career post in administration. Her determination to 'prove myself in a hostile environment' eventually led to her appointment as head of a university department.

Professional conflict

The women described their own professional experience in terms of relationships between themselves as women, and masculine institutions or male colleagues. This was particularly true of those who are or have been involved in (often very bitter) conflict with their institutions about their own career progress. Those who said they had been encouraged by men at early stages of their career had found, in common with women in industry and in other male-dominated professions, that their ambition for positions of real institutional power had eventually attracted antagonism: 'Senior men get Brownie points for encouraging the careers of junior women, but it's different when you're on a level with them.'

Those in obviously feminist areas of work felt this had increased professional conflict. Others, even in mainstream academic subjects, saw antagonism towards their career progression as a direct consequence of their being women seeking positions of institutional power.

Two of the women spontaneously mentioned the effect of working with a high proportion of male colleagues who were Catholic (in one case due to geography and in another to subject area). They felt this reinforced sexist antagonism towards them, as professional women. One described the cultural barrier as 'not so much banging your head against a glass ceiling as grappling with a smoke screen.' The fact that the source might be incense made it no easier to cope with.

Institutional responsibility

Some of the women described aspects of accelerated promotion at early stages in their academic career, although only two described them as problematic. Such moves had been the consequence of changes in institutional structure, or the coincidental retirement of a number of senior colleagues – an increasing phenomenon as the 1960s staffing bulge made its way through the institutions. Some also associated rapid promotion with the positive attitudes of senior officers towards equal opportunities in their institutions. (A number of these officers themselves could be classified as cultural 'outsiders', either because they were women or, more often, by virtue of their origins outside the United Kingdom.) Unfortunately these positive attitudes had not always been backed up by the training, counselling or mentoring any relatively inexperienced staff member needed on promotion to management level.

The main drawbacks of accelerated promotion in any career structure can include:

- insufficient management experience for the degree of responsibility, often revealed in poor decision-making skills and inadequacy in dealing with people and their problems;
- inexperience in policy-making;
- limited experience of formal committee work and the informal work that underpins it; .
- lack of a network of mentors and contacts in powerful positions, internally and externally;
- jealousy among contemporaries and former peers;
- escalation of family–career conflicts when the individuals, their partners and families have insufficient time for structural and psychological adjustment to each new level of career demand.

These are not failings associated with women only. They are typical of people who have not been adequately prepared for the level of responsibility given to them, and who have insufficient institutional support. The effects are often emphasized in the case of women because they are more isolated than men at management levels: unless they are blessed with a particularly high proportion of generous colleagues they are likely to have less opportunity for informal support than their male colleagues.

Such support is not only helpful in day-to-day work, but can be critical during selection for promotion. Two of the women described selection interviews at various times that had left them feeling that, 'If they're as unpleasant as this I don't want to work with them', and 'You can stuff your lousy job.'

Candidates who seek promotion seldom feel encouraged to complain about hostile selection procedures when they balance the disruption caused by a formal complaint against what they may hope to gain. Mentors and networks can provide support for the individual; furthermore, an institution that has implemented a system of formal mentors may be sufficiently alert to the problems of discrimination to address them through the training of senior staff and monitoring of appointments and promotions.

Authority and identity

Some of the women interviewed described the behaviour of female colleagues that undermined both personal and collective energy in the work for change. Such behaviour was not uncommon at meetings among women who wanted the benefits of change but who, for a variety of reasons, would not commit themselves to working for it. They spent time and energy arguing why suggestions would not work, instead of helping to identify and implement possible improvements. They appeared to be locked into academic-type displays of individual intellectual machismo: 'My argument is stronger than yours.' The result undermined the efforts of colleagues if it threatened the common gender identity that underpins joint and individual confidence.

This paralysis seems to be the result of internal conflict between personal ambition, professional identity and institutional authority. However unsatisfactory the status quo is, it is the source of an academic's institutional authority and underpins professional identity. This can be a real dilemma for women who feel that, from school onwards, they have always had to work harder for recognition than their male contemporaries. What happens when that authority is fundamentally challenged? And what does it mean if they themselves challenge the source of the hard-won professional authority that they value so highly? For some this is too painful a question to think about, yet they cannot move beyond it. They attend meetings to identify possible answers, which they are bound to find unacceptable, especially if the whole question is also bound up with challenges to male authority in their personal lives.

To consider effective strategies for change entails dethroning the gods: demystifying the laying-on of hands that ensures the academic succession. One professor said in interview, 'Women often find it easier to blame themselves' [for their lack of further promotion].

To deconstruct a myth before you are sure that you have a better one to substitute takes the same kind of intellectual courage that characterizes good research and scholarship. The difference is that for academic women considering women's academic careers the process cannot be distanced by conventions of objectivity. Their personal lives are at the very centre of the thinking process.

What greater commitment does the profession expect?

Bibliography

Brittan, A. (1989) *Masculinity and Power*. Oxford, Blackwell.
Bourner, T., Reynolds, A., Hamed, M. and Barnett, R. (1991) *Part-Time Students and their Experience of Higher Education*. Buckingham, SRHE/Open University Press.

Connell, R. (1987) *Gender and Power.* Cambridge, Polity Press.

Duke, C. (1992) *The Learning University: Towards a New Paradigm?* Buckingham, SRHE/Open University Press.

Giddens, A. (1992) *The Transformation of Intimacy: Sexuality, Love and Eroticism in Modern Societies.* Cambridge, Polity Press.

Spurling, A. (1990) *Report of the Women in Higher Education Research Project: 1988–90.* Cambridge, King's College Research Centre.

Taylor, P. (1992) Ethnic group data and applications to higher education, *Higher Education Quarterly*, 46, 4, Autumn.

Thompson, A. and Wilcox, H. (1989) *Teaching Women: Feminism and English Studies.* Manchester, Manchester University Press.

Tight, M. (1991) *Higher Education: A Part-Time Perspective.* Buckingham, Open University Press.

Wilson, B. and Byrne, E. (1987) *Women in the University: A Policy Report.* Queensland, University of Queensland Press.

5

On Becoming and Being a Manager in Education

Janet Powney

It hardly seems appropriate in one's 'prime' – or as others might say, 'having reached a certain age' to still be reflecting on how I became the only female head of department in a polytechnic and what it was like doing that job in a male-oriented institution for several years before another woman was appointed at the same level. During this period only one woman was more senior for perhaps five years, being a Dean and then Assistant Director before leaving education. Working now in a predominantly female organization has helped me to consolidate views on management in educational institutions in the UK, views which fit rather well with my own research experiences and much of the literature on equal opportunities. Maybe the climate has changed, and if I were starting my educational career now rather than more than 30 years ago, I would find circumstances more encouraging to women and other groups in a minority in senior positions in the hierarchy. This chapter considers some of the factors in attempting to become a manager and then fulfilling the role which affect any possibility of redressing this imbalance. As well as referring to recent papers I shall be drawing on my own experience and extensively on the findings of a small-scale research project funded by the European Commission which aimed to draw on the experience of women and black and ethnic minority managers in educational institutions.

The hesitancy expressed in these opening sentences mirrors the frustrations and uncertainty being experienced by other women in becoming and being managers in education establishments. What I am sure about is that being a member of a minority group at any level is special; social interactions will be different if you are female and/or black in a predominantly white male environment. No doubt the converse could also be true for white men in a predominantly female and/or black environment – but there are no such organizations in education in the UK currently; in all our mainstream educational organizations, men dominate and control resources. This is reprehensible not least because teaching oversees the foundation of everyone's career, and therefore developments in the ethos, authority and role models purveyed by teacher education are of supreme importance.

As teacher training and other HE institutions emerge from nearly two decades of reorganization of structures, institutions, curricula, financial arrangements and governance, the result is that monotechnic, single-sex training colleges, the bastions of teacher training with their formidable principals, have been merged beyond recognition into institutions training other professionals and academics. Christine Heward (1992) tracks four periods in staffing of teacher training, including the earliest period dominated by male clerics and a period, 1910–1960, when women were dominant: 'their authority legitimated by academic qualifications, the prevalence of sex segregated institutions and the Board of Education regulations.' Heward argues that the latter was part of the strategy of the Liberal government elected in 1906 to reduce the power of the Church of England. Women took on principalships – primarily of the segregated women's colleges – and dominated teacher training until the rapid expansion of teacher training to cope with the postwar influx of men to the profession later facilitated by the dramatic expansion in teacher training in the 1960s. As more men became teachers from the 1950s on, so women's authority in the profession has been eroded. Now initial teacher education is just one of the areas within large diverse colleges and universities 'in which managerial authority, seen as overwhelmingly masculine, is legitimated' (Heward, 1992).

Becoming a manager in education

By analysing the life histories of some 40 members of under-represented groups who have nevertheless achieved senior positions, the project reported in *Outside of the Norm* (Powney and Weiner, 1992) explored the personal and institutional obstacles experienced by women and members of black and/or ethnic minorities in their attempts to become and remain managers. It also explained why some women are opting out of management as a career strategy. For example, from a position outside the senior hierarchy, a black female academic explained her inability to engage in standard management practices:

> university management structures are highly middle class, white and male dominated . . . [I find myself] as a black working class woman outside of the norm of being acceptable on three counts: class, race and gender.
>
> (Powney and Weiner, 1992: 40)

Participants in the project also suggested management strategies in educational institutions, including higher education, that enhance the promotion of women and black and/or ethnic minority men and women. Although the project team aimed to identify the most senior manager in each organization, it is significant that it was sometimes necessary to go some way down the hierarchy to find an informant working in education who was black and/or from an ethnic minority, especially among men. The members of the group who were interviewed had in common sufficient professional experience of educational management and its structures to be able to communicate how it feels to be in a senior position and the struggle (or not) they had to get there. The research team was thus able to accumulate a shared perspective on the factors necessary to achieve career success and what it is like to have managerial responsibility when you are from a group under-represented in senior management and in educational institutions generally. It was felt that these views would be particularly helpful to others developing policies and practices for their personal and institutional development.

Evidence already mentioned shows that women, including individuals from black and ethnic minority groups, are under-represented as managers in all sectors of education. Sutherland (1991) suggests that one reason might be that women are not often seen in positions of authority and therefore are not considered when appointments to such positions are made. Commonly held attitudes which prejudice the appointment of women to senior positions include the following:

- women seem incongruous in occupations where we are accustomed to seeing men;
- it is asserted that men would not work for a female boss;
- going further, it is argued that women also prefer to have a man rather than a woman in authority.

One could apply this equally to ethnic minorities, as many white men and women would find it unusual, and from their point of view undesirable, to have a member of a black ethnic minority group in a position of authority.

There is also evidence that equal opportunities policies are increasingly being developed for educational institutions in the 1990s (Feather and Russell, 1990; Taylor, 1990). All advertisements for posts in higher education carry tags such as 'We are an equal opportunities employer'. What this means in practice varies from institution to institution as we discovered from an ESRC project, 'Developing Equitable Staff Policies in FE and HE (1991–94)' (published as Farish *et al.*, 1995). Institutions can be viewed as being located on a continuum of adoption of, or involvement with, equal opportunities in relation to staff. The continuum can also be represented diagrammatically, as shown in Figure 5.1.

An institution with an ethos of equal opportunities is one, for instance, where there is awareness of the full range of obstacles barring individual progress and where every attempt has been made to remove such obstacles (Powney and Weiner, 1992). At the other end of the continuum, lip-service

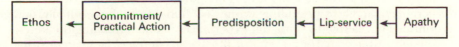

Figure 5.1   Continuum of institutional involvement with equal opportunities

institutions only make tokenistic nods towards equality issues and in the final category, 'apathy', there is little evidence of any awareness or adherence to equality issues. Organizations with a commitment to practical action are improving their recruitment, selection and appointment procedures and their staff development policies. Appraisal schemes are also important in drawing attention to staff whose careers might otherwise be overlooked.

At present, there are white women as well as black and ethnic minority men and women who have achieved senior positions in their colleges and universities and in so doing have gathered experiences and learnt strategies which are of value to others in similar positions or to institutions which have a commitment to eradicating sexist and racist bias. In our EC project we believed that one way forward was to draw on the experiences of this group of people in devising change strategies. Only one of our white female informants reported no disadvantaging experiences on account of her gender.

How did those women who are senior managers in education get there?

One of the prevalent excuses given for male pre-eminence in management posts is that female candidates rarely put themselves forward. Let us leave aside the self-justificatory nature of this reason and consider some of the factors which encourage women to apply for promotion and the personal and institutional obstacles they perceive in even taking this first step. Our informants were all successful by definition and their suggested reasons for success can be summarized in terms of:

• personal motivation and support;
• being on an appropriate springboard for promotion; and
• learning strategies to cope with personal and institutional discrimination encountered in their careers.

Factors identified in the career process may be shared by all managers but difficulties are amplified, and certainly not simplified, by being a woman and/or from an ethnic minority. The first step for all managerial aspirants is to have sufficient confidence to apply for promotion rather than to await recognition, as many women in particular seem to do. Common factors in the careers of the senior managers in our study included a supportive framework from their parents, family, friends or community. Working-class informants especially reported the help from their parents in 'establishing an ambitious climate', as one person said. Families therefore help to develop personal confidence. Professional confidence can only be built up by experience. I take an eclectic theoretical view that we do not develop in isolation but are socially constructed, learning behaviours and attitudes which are determined largely by prevailing attitudes at home and school initially, and confirmed or rejected by our adult experiences. Women fulfilling the lowest status jobs, often on part-time and/or short-term contracts, lack career structures and 'clout' and are constantly having their lowliness reinforced.

Senior managers in a variety of educational organisations suggested the following strategies to those who want to gain promotion:

- Hard work, persistence, patience and staying power.
- Get qualified.
- Have confidence in your own ability.
- Maintain a sense of humour.

- Be aware that sexism and racism can affect your career.
- Don't lose your balance over sexist comments.
- Get support from: peers, tutors, networks, family, other professionals.

- Networking, nurturing and self-consciousness: these are all important strategies.
- Be instrumental; learn from others.
- Blame the system for negative experiences, not always yourself.

- As a manager, learn to pare things down to what is really important.
- Use all strategies, learn the rules of the system and play them.
- Learn discretion; 'when is it worth battering an issue or behaving covertly'.
- Work out and utilise strengths of others and how to learn to compensate for weakness.
- Get better at decoding written messages: 'Women tend to see blame where not intended and men see praise where not intended'.
- If developments cannot be achieved co-operatively, they should either be dropped, delayed or other methods of achieving change explored.

- Develop the courage to promote yourself; do not be squeamish.
- Take risks and seize opportunities; sometimes these might entail a change of direction or having a higher profile in an institution.
- Part of a feminist commitment must be to take up the challenges and compromises of management. Women should therefore go for influential positions.

- APPLY for good positions.

Figure 5.2 Admonitions to would-be managers
(Source: adapted from *Outside of the Norm*, Powney and Weiner, revised edition, 1992.)

Self-confidence was identified as the key to becoming and remaining a manager and those with the longest experience tended to be more relaxed; for example, a senior administrator said she now had the self-confidence to use any strategy, even accepting being mistaken on the telephone for being the secretary, without being overly strident or assertive. One very senior academic woman said that having a daughter had given her confidence. Informants frequently reiterated this need for self-confidence and it figured largely in the 'admonitions to would-be managers' listed in Figure 5.2; material factors were also important, and it was not easy for some to acquire this confidence, especially if they came from a working-class background.

Many informants of working-class origin reported feeling 'out of place'

and unsure of their abilities even after many years of successful professional
life and of having more than minimum academic qualifications. Findings
suggest that there are those who make their working-class and/or ethnic background an advantage, using it to give them support; and others who, perhaps,
do not or cannot use their family or community as a source of strength. White
women with working-class backgrounds were most likely to express the tensions between women traditionally putting home and children first and pursuing a career. As one of our white female informants put it:

> Part of women's conditioning is not to question a man's right to have a
> career whereas for a woman, each career moves her further and further
> outside what is seen as a conventional role.

(Powney and Weiner, 1992)

Whereas men are often constrained by having to earn sufficient to provide
for dependants, women are more likely also to engage in the practical side
of caring – arranging meals, shopping, baby sitting, looking after the elderly,
etc. These time-consuming activities leave little time after work for developing networks of friends, and refreshing other parts of one's personal development. A senior woman administrator at Oxbridge told me that outside work
she has no time for other friendships as the family is so demanding on her
time: 'I have so little time for them, that they have to have it all.' (This informant also considered that many, not all men, find it necessary to 'hide
behind a facade of being utterly efficient and utterly competent all the time.'
She felt they do not have to consider home affairs because someone else is
running the home for them or they do not admit it because they think it will
reduce their stature.)

Upward mobility requires an appropriate springboard and a major
obstacle is getting to the appropriate position from which it is reasonable to
apply for a senior post. Conventional 'careers' equate hierarchical advancement of career with promotion rather than sideways moves. As a woman the
convention is to apply for only a modest advancement. Where terms of
approval such as 'go-ahead', 'on the fast track' and 'ambitious' may be used
of men applying for posts two or more jumps ahead of their current position,
negative terms are used of women in the same position: 'assertive', 'aggressive', 'strident', 'pushy' are examples of terms used disapprovingly. So
women tend to move up a hierarchy slowly and may get blocked from getting
to the penultimate position which therefore precludes them from becoming
top executives. However, top women in universities have been able to use
networking to reinforce their future applications. This proved especially
effective for three women who were encouraged by their contacts from
undergraduate and postgraduate days at Oxbridge to apply for senior positions there. I suspect it is just as much an advantage to women as to men to
have attended university at Oxford or Cambridge.

It is less common in educational circles than it is in managerial branches
of other professions for individuals to seek out a mentor but it is a strategy
highly recommended by our project informants. The most obvious difficulty

is finding a suitable mentor – one who is senior enough in the profession, if not in the same institution, to provide appropriate advice and to encourage access to career opportunities. There are few enough women and members of ethnic minorities in such advantageous positions. Those who are there do not always identify with, or feel any responsibility towards, such groups lower down the scale. Our previous prime minister was a case in point: women's prospects in employment deteriorated during her term of office. Mentors are more likely to be found among white male managers who have benefited from the status quo. They may well find difficulty in suggesting anything other than their own strategy in getting promotion, a strategy which may not be accessible to others because of their gender or colour.

Being a black woman brings double indemnity. There are so few women from ethnic minorities in higher education that one has to seek explanations from those in springboard positions, such as school teaching which is often a precursor to jobs in higher education. In the *Outside of the Norm* project, black informants, men and women, reported various discriminatory experiences which, they perceived, had impeded their career progression, for example:

- being set-up for a job which had already been earmarked for someone else or where there seemed to be an implicit colour bar;
- job applications from black applicants which went missing;
- a local education authority adviser giving a black female teacher misleading criteria applicable for secondment to study for a higher degree;
- several examples of black candidates having to make a seemingly inordinate number of applications before obtaining promotion. For example, one man from an ethnic minority group applied for 19 deputy posts before getting one, and then put in 120 headship applications before being interviewed for three, all of which he was offered.

In some cases it seemed that promotion opportunities were deliberately blocked by line managers through providing poor references or by suggesting to candidates that they were not yet ready for promotion. Ironically in the light of public policies to recruit more black staff, one informant thought that his headteacher had blocked his career advancement *because* he provided black representation within the staffing body which could not be replaced easily. This is an obvious example of tokenism, where the appointment of women or black and ethnic minority staff is a political strategy rather than an indication of either a genuine institutional commitment to equal opportunities or a belief in the individual's suitability. This can lead to considerable overload for managers from under-represented groups in all organizations. They face the dilemma of refusing to join committees and working parties because they already have a full work load when at the same time that decision means there will continue to be no minority representation on that group. As one of our black female informants succinctly put it: 'when the institution finds a "good black", everybody wants you.' Similar situations encountered included what one informant referred to as a 'twofer' – a black woman can fill two committee positions at once: as a member of an ethnic minority group and as a female senior manager. Thus two categories of an institution's equal opportunities policy can be filled by a single person.

Women and especially those from ethnic minorities may have to face blatant hostility from colleagues. A woman who eventually became a secondary headteacher was so startled and enraged by sexism at headship level, evidenced in comments from male headteachers working in the same authority such as, 'The role of a woman teaching is not to be a head', that she kept a 'little blue book' of examples of sexist attitudes of colleagues, peers, parents and 'outsiders'. She was the only female headteacher of a secondary school employed by the authority when she was appointed in the late 1980s, and has gone on to be a senior member of the union executive, to take a leading role in a quango and been given an OBE along the way.

Black colleagues are constantly challenged by racial hostility, both blatant and more subtle, meted out by white men and women. It is now difficult to be overtly racist and remain within the law; nevertheless, there is still occasionally blatant professional racism such as a headteacher telling a new appointment that she (the head) had been upset when she saw he was black. Another example quoted was that of a black woman teacher being asked at an earlier stage of her career why, as a black woman, she was working in a boys' school. The same question was not asked of white female staff. Yet again, a black senior inspector in a local education authority was obliged to do her own secretarial work for eight months as the allocated secretary refused to work for her; white female colleagues of equivalent rank, appointed at the same time, were allocated personal assistants as well as secretaries.

Many women – though not, it should be noted, all – have a struggle to reach managerial positions in higher education and in the career stages leading up to a post in a university or college of higher education.

Being a manager

In spite of applications for senior positions by women and non-white groups being frequently blocked because they do not have the prior requirement of middle management status, some do make it to the top of departments and of large organizations. Unfortunately their struggles may not stop there. They share the problems and uncertainties that all managers have whatever their gender or colour, and have additional difficulties because of their gender or colour. For example, those who eventually achieve senior status report feelings of high visibility and believe that they are often treated merely as representatives of an (under-represented) group, as evidenced by continual requests to be a token presence on senior committees (Bangar and McDermott, 1989). Women also report feelings of isolation and loneliness and frequently perceive their workplace as male-dominated, hostile and contradictory (Marshall, 1987).

Isolation and high visibility

What is it like being a manager if you can never be a member of the dominant group, white males? Those who experience racial or gender prejudice in attempts to reach a senior position may continue to experience discrimination, albeit in different forms, when they do become managers. Hostility, exploitation and patronage may continue in subtle forms but are exacerbated by the isolation of managers mentioned earlier. For all managers, a high degree of isolation goes with the job. Most managers feel it necessary to distance themselves to some extent from their subordinate staff. However, women and ethnic minorities face a double loss, being separated from their own support group without at the same time being able to replace it with another among senior management colleagues when most of these are white males.

High visibility also goes with the job if you are one of the few women or ethnic minority members; your statements seem to be interpreted as having come from a woman, not just from another colleague. High visibility is a strategy common among conventional male managers, of constructing competence through public performance. This is a proactive stance, likely to get one noticed and to give one advantage in a managerial and increasingly entrepreneurial career structure which favours the articulate, forceful and confident. Members of under-represented groups, especially those from ethnic minorities, need take no action to become highly visible once they are managers; on the contrary, they may have to take evasive action. Several of our project informants reported that their high visibility put them under intense pressure not to fail. As a black woman said, 'any weakness in performance would be more glaring than any achievements, success she brings to the job.'

Another woman, also black, rejected a job because she felt that everyone was waiting to see her 'fall flat on her face' and a white senior manager reported that she 'always felt that most of my male colleagues were just waiting for me to put a foot wrong.' It is worth commenting here that isolated, high visibility may be particularly uncomfortable for the large majority of women who generally prefer flatter, more participatory styles of management, more open to change and with a greater ability to work collaboratively (Marshall, 1985). Jenny Corbett conveyed her surprise at being in a high profile position in higher education compared to her previous career in special education and as a wife and mother:

> I still feel slightly strange, now that I am playing in so contrasting a context. It is as if the stigma of experiencing that female invisibility now makes my current visibility in higher education appear fraudulent. I often feel I am in the wrong play with a script for which I have not rehearsed.
>
> (Corbett, 1992: 242)

In summarizing individuals' experiences in becoming and being educational managers, in *Outside of the Norm*, we said,

The most depressing message is that actions of discrimination and promotion of unequal opportunities are rife among the best educated
people and most senior education institutions in the land. It is evident
that complacency and bad practice abound. . . .

(Powney and Weiner, 1992: 31)

The kinds of poor practice that we had in mind were not in stated policies
but rather in the absence of explicit policy and supporting procedures which
would discourage exploitation and patronage and enable women to take a
full role in the management of their organization.

Exploitation and patronage

Exploitation of managers may seem a curious notion, but I am interested
here in 'deputies', in the one backing up the top executive. My hunch is that
women *are allowed to* rise to being deputies in a department, faculty, or whole
institution and are seen as evidence that there is an equal opportunities
policy in operation. AUT reports (such as AUT, 1992) show that such
deputies are likely to be paid less than men of comparable status but exploitation probably goes beyond that. The caricature expressed in conversation
among women and in cartoons is that an idea initially expressed by a woman
only becomes recognized and appreciated when a man says it. Senior white
male colleagues may support a woman's rise through the ranks, and there
are many examples of such patronage. But there is a cost: eternal gratitude
from the recipient who is rarely allowed to surpass the patron's status.

One example reported in *Outside of the Norm* was of a woman who decided
to publish an edited book of articles which had appeared over several years
in a journal she alone had edited. Her boss would only agree to the publication if his name was on the cover – a suggestion which she rejected. This
is echoed time and again by our female informants who felt their ideas had
been taken over and 'owned' by senior, male colleagues.

Of course the greatest exploitation is institutionally, and indeed nation-
ally, sanctioned by incentives to employ untenured, part-time staff members
over quite long periods on successive contracts, thus depriving them of
career and economic benefits. Most of the women who had followed their
husband's career wherever it took the family (i.e., about a quarter of our
white informants) tended to have had this experience. Of 11 white women
interviewed by one researcher in *Outside of the Norm*, seven had followed their
husband's career. One had worked in 18 countries across all five continents,
moving with her husband's job. The careers of all seven of these women had
been affected as they had lost substantial professional ground after each
move.

There are so many ways in which even as a senior manager one still meets
racism or sexism through being patronized. For example, a difficult form of
racism to combat is the patronizing attitude of white colleagues who appear

surprised if a black person runs a meeting efficiently or speaks well at a conference. As a black female informant said, 'Their expectations are so low that when you outstrip their expectations, they turn around and become almost a fan.'

Peripheralizing women's contribution is a continuing and effective way for the dominant group to maintain their advantage. How often are women put in charge of resource committees or are even members of such powerful groups? They are more likely to find themselves convening the equal opportunities working party, a learning and teaching development group, a curriculum development team – hard working and supportive groups in the organization but groups which are unlikely to have sufficient power to be subversive or to have radical effects on the institution.

For many years, I did not appreciate the extent to which I was being patronized. The following relatively trivial incident occurred about 18 months before I left my polytechnic and I believe it was instrumental in my seeking premature voluntary redundancy from that organization. It illustrates the kind of patronizing attitudes that can still surprise and shock women managers. After nearly 20 years in higher education, I had considerable experience and expertise in course design and evaluation, having been on various CNAA boards and working parties as well as having been a course leader and subsequently head of department responsible for research and development. I had a good working knowledge of various levels in the organization. I was then 'entrusted' with the task of developing a modular diploma scheme across the institution which could subsequently be converted into a modular degree. I put the quotation marks around entrusted because it was an extremely difficult task to convince other departments to participate since it would involve their giving up some of their autonomy in some aspects of timetabling and resources. There was also verbal senior management support for the project, although initially with little apparent understanding of the practical implications. Eventually, the programme staggered into its first cohort of 80-odd students chasing courses over five of the polytechnic sites. The following year, recruitment was over 100 undergraduates and we were planning the top-up degree year. At about this time, at the end of a formal academic board meeting (at which I was one of the, by then, two female heads of department), the Rector announced he wished, after the formal business was completed, to give me a vote of thanks. Expecting some recognition of at least the hard work, if not the skill, I had demonstrated in implementing the new scheme, I was dumbstruck to hear him announce to the assembly that I had made a great contribution to the polytechnic by providing him (personally) with a new kitten! The statement was not inaccurate, as he had one of the litter as had one of the secretaries in my department, but I do not think he understood the inauspicious timing and content of the message he was sending out to the rest of the polytechnic. Whether his action was ignorant or wilful, it completely undermined much of the struggle towards equal opportunities in that organization. It summed up in a few seconds the chief executive's approach to senior female colleagues. In retrospect, I regret that I did not have the awareness, wit, facility and confidence to challenge even in a humorous way a statement which would never have been made about a man in the same circumstances.

The future

I would like to be optimistic about women's opportunities as managers in higher education. After all there is now legislation to support equal opportunities and all universities are formally equal opportunities employers. The major hazard remains, I think, in the lack of awareness of discriminatory practices. Until recently much of university life has been inward looking, concerned with scholarship, emphasizing academic freedom of the individual lecturer and of the university itself. Collegiality tends to recreate the status quo.

> Their self image as fair minded people has proved a real problem to get over in the universities. You are working against the grain of people who feel they have been fair all their lives and couldn't possibly . . . they don't have the understanding of things like indirect discrimination. It's just not a concept they acknowledge.
>
> (Powney and Weiner, 1992: 20)

The black woman who said this had worked in two universities and concluded that there was something peculiar to the culture of university departments which limited both the potential of individual staff and of the implementation of equal opportunities.

> University management structures are highly middle class, white and male dominated which fosters a culture that supports the old public school boy network.
>
> (ibid.)

The possibility that they might be discriminatory is anathema to university vice-chancellors and yet the evidence of direct discrimination is there in the AUT report (AUT, 1992) referred to earlier. Managers we interviewed had experienced open hostility. Women informants expressed a general discomfort about conflict, especially with men who behaved aggressively to female management. One way of coping with this was to be almost over-prepared to feel in thorough command of their work, partly because this boosted their self-confidence and partly because they did not want to be caught out. This takes a lot of time but as one of our top managers said, 'I never let them know that.'

It is not enough for individual women to strive against sexism in their efforts to become managers and be effective in that role. Institutional policies and practice must support those individuals. Having an explicit and meaningful equal opportunities policy is only the first step. The key is in implementing proper staff recruitment, appointment and promotion procedures backed up by effective appraisal schemes and a coherent staff development programme. This view is reinforced by Heward and Taylor (1992) who showed that the unimpressive progress in the implementation of equal opportunities policies in British higher education founders at the stage of monitoring recruitment practices. Other factors which encourage women to get to the appropriate springboard for promotion and then to fulfil managerial functions are flexi-time, opportunities for part-time working and job sharing, crèche facilities and career-break packages. Add to these encouragement for a mentor system and networking within and outside the organization, and a university will have good management practices for all its employees regardless of gender or ethnic background.

We should not be perpetuating a system where women feel excluded from university management structures because they are outside of the norm in terms of their gender. However, the reality is continuing tension between the economic pressures and competitive environment of the 1990s and even legislative equal opportunities requirements. Women need more than legislation. They need the springboard of opportunity to become a manager. They need effective institutional non-discriminatory practices to enable their organizations to gain the maximum benefit from their appointment.

Bibliography

AUT (1991) *Pay at the Top of the University Ladder: Results of a Survey of Professional and Senior Staff Salaries in UK Universities.* London, AUT.

AUT (1992) *Sex Discrimination in Universities: Report of an Academic Audit Carried out by AUT Research Department.* London, AUT.

Bangar, S. and McDermott, J. (1989) 'Black women speak' in F. Widdowson Migniuolo and H. De Lyon (eds) *Women Teachers: Issues and Experiences.* Milton Keynes, Open University Press.

Corbett, J. (1992) 'Careful teaching: researching a special career.' *British Education Research Journal*, 8(3), 235–43.

Engender (1995) *Gender Audit 1995: Putting Scottish Women in the Picture.* Edinburgh, Engender.

Equal Opportunities Commission (1994) *Labour Market Structures and Prospects for Women.* University of Warwick, Equal Opportunities Commission.

Farish, M., McPake, J., Powney, J. and Weiner, G. (1995) *Equal Opportunities in Colleges and Universities*, Buckingham, SRHE/Open University Press.

Feather, D. and Russell, T. S. (1990) 'A management course for women teachers'. *Women in Management*, 5(5), 7–10.

Heward, C. (1992) Men and women and the rise of professional society: the intriguing history of teacher educators, paper presented at the annual conference of the British Educational Research Association, University of Stirling, September.

Heward, C. and Taylor, P. (1992) 'Women at the top in higher education: equal opportunities policies in action?' *Policy and Politics*, 20(2), 111–21.

Marshall, J. (1987) Less equal than others, *The Times Educational Supplement*, 17 April.

Marshall, C. (1985) 'From culturally defined to self defined: career stages of women administrators'. *Journal of Educational Thought*, 19(2), 134–47.

Powney, J. (1994) 'Power in education – the changing context of gender research', keynote address, Gender and Education Research Network, Glasgow.

Powney, J. and Weiner, G. (1992) (revised edition) *Outside of the Norm.* London, University of the South Bank.

Sutherland, M. (1991) 'Women and education: progress and problems'. *Prospects,* XXI, 2.

Taylor, H. (1990) 'Management development for black teachers'. *Women in Management,* 5(5), 15–17.

Weiner, G. (1994) *Feminism in Education: an Introduction.* Buckingham, Open University Press.

6

Black Afro-Caribbean Women in Higher Education in the United Kingdom, from the 1950s to the 1990s

Joceyln Barrow

Introduction

The ability of Afro-Caribbean women to persevere and succeed in a hostile society against all the odds which they face, coupled with a resilience which then becomes inbred over time and passed on to their female relations and offspring, is extremely well documented in numerous sociological publications, both in the UK and, of course, in the United States.

For the most part their progress follows a similar path in the USA and UK, especially with regard to those entering these two countries in the late 1950s and early 1960s. One of the principal reasons for leaving the Caribbean in the first place was to seek access to those higher education opportunities which were not available within the confines of a highly colonized group of islands, in the throes of seeking to combine to form the type of political federation, free from colonization, which could have assisted them in attracting the necessary funding for expansion.

The fact that there existed at that time the University College of the West Indies, as an affiliated College of London University, whose main campus was based at Mona, Jamaica, with one of the world's most renowned agricultural institutions located on the St Augustine Campus in Trinidad, did little to satisfy the numbers of individuals for whom diversity beckoned. The war effort of the 1940s had provided employment abroad for men in many cases. The young women left behind had little choice other than to become domestic servants, nurses in the local hospitals, or to work in cottage industries, with just a few attempting to go beyond these areas in the one or two teacher training colleges or junior civil service posts which then existed.

The persistence of young women in the 1950s and 1960s in seeking to perform as well as young men has to be seen in the context of the fact that, where further and higher education was concerned, any spare money that families had was seen as being better spent on improving the lot of men, rather than the young women. Because of this, there was an implicit understanding by the women that the work which was available to them had to be viewed as a necessary stepping stone to saving the money required to improve their lot abroad.

What is not widely recognized is the fact that education in these islands, most especially the British West Indian islands, copied that of British educational institutions. Depending upon one's family circumstances, an individual could achieve at primary, intermediate, and secondary levels. Young girls could take satisfaction from the fact that if they completed at least the intermediate level, they had a realistic chance of becoming employable. At secondary level, to this day, the standard of education is hardly ever equalled by their counterparts in similar institutions abroad. Thus, those individuals who made the transatlantic crossing, having aspired to and achieved their potential at this level, found themselves to be competing at standards equal to or better than their British counterparts. The confidence which this inspired is part and parcel of the success story of many of these young women, who, unlike what we euphemistically call today 'Black British' young people, retained vestiges of their own culture which has stood them in good stead.

It is here that the story really begins of the perceived and actual successes of various individuals who made this 'crossing', bears witness to the determination found in black Afro-Caribbean women, who have chosen to remain in the field of education. For the purposes of this chapter, I have chosen to present the evidence in the form of case studies of women who have been highly successful in their specific roles, at every point in their extremely diverse careers. Most significant are the similarities in their reasons for pursuing this particular form of personal advancement, which stemmed from an innate belief that given their vision of what 'ought' to be taking place with regard to the advancement of the Afro-Caribbean community which they found on arrival, they could most certainly 'do better'.

Case studies

L

L arrived in the UK from Jamaica in the 1950s, after having served in the Jamaican Civil Service, in the Department of Inland Revenue. Having also worked as a volunteer for the YWCA in Jamaica, she sought to continue this work with young people in the YWCA (UK), on her arrival, becoming closely involved with the organization by completing a research project on their behalf.

To establish the credibility of her work with young people, L decided to pursue a first degree in sociology, and went on to gain postgraduate qualifications in youth work as well as an Advanced Academic Diploma in Education. Her later Master's degree in public policy and administration focused specifically on the issue of race relations, as applied to the Youth Service and the concerns of the youth of both the Afro-Caribbean and Asian populations in the UK.

Her reputation in the field of education and youth work was further enhanced when, recognizing the fact that a gap existed, she chose to lecture at university level to individuals whose decisions affected these young people. L's reputation in lecturing in the field of race relations and social policies, as well as her decision to run training courses for youth and community workers, teachers, postgraduate students, magistrates and voluntary organisations, is well-established.

Coincidentally, at this point i.e., the late 1960s and early 1970s, the politically sensitive issue of multi-culturalism in British schools and other educational establishments took hold. Her former activities found her extremely well-prepared to participate in the dialogue which ensued. More importantly, as a consultant in the work of a number of voluntary and statutory bodies in many local authorities across the country, she has been consistently called upon to advise on a number of new equal opportunities policies, assisting in designing training modules in this area of work, as well as conducting in-service training programmes for institutions and education authorities alike. Again recognizing a gap to be filled, L turned her sights to initiating staff development programmes at FE college-based levels, contributing at the same time to youth and community service policies at county level, eventually becoming a County Equal Opportunity Officer.

As will be seen from the other case studies in this chapter, the need to be *actively* involved in working with students was never far from her work profile. L made a conscious decision to commit herself to teaching on the social studies/sociology courses at FE college level, whenever possible. Working as a Student Services Officer, with overall responsibility for the Students' Advisory Service, also became an integral part of that work profile, as did becoming an area youth officer and careers advisory officer in areas where there was a high density population of minority ethnic groups.

The progression from involvement at the local authority level to working at the public service appointments level, in order to distil these high-profile skills in the area of multi-culturalism and youth work generally, would seem to be a natural one; and one for which a certain degree of preparedness, ability and assertiveness on the part of an individual from a minority ethnic group was absolutely essential. Again, the progression into the European education arena, in Denmark, Holland and Belgium in particular, on behalf of particular local education authorities in the UK, raised an international perspective which has been beneficial not only to herself, but to all those with whom she has subsequently come into contact.

Being in the right place at the right time, in the developing world of resolving increasing racial tension, by utilizing education as a most powerful means by which to do so, meant that L was frequently called upon to assist in associated areas which involved the youth of the UK, such as the probation service, the magistracy and, increasingly and less contentiously perhaps, the arts.

During the entire development of her career to date, which has now expanded to her becoming a salaried officer in an extremely high-profile central government public service organization, L has maintained close links with her country of origin, Jamaica. She has been instrumental in the setting-up of advice/consultation groups on issues which affect young Jamaican nationals in the UK, as well as those at home in the West Indies, with a view to the continued improvement of these young people in the international arena.

H

H, also born in Jamaica, achieved passes at secondary school up to Senior Cambridge Examination level at high school; and worked for a while in a junior post in the Civil Service, before deciding to pursue her higher education in the UK.

Her route to higher education was somewhat different, in that she chose to match the qualifications of her British peers by acquiring GCE 'O' and 'A' level passes. Then, unusually, H decided, for economic reasons mainly, to find employment before continuing on her chosen route in higher education. This first period of employment took place in several different settings: first as a deputy head of section in the cost office of a local council in one of London's most cosmopolitan boroughs; then as a clerical assistant in a tax office; next, as a bookkeeper in a catering company, and finally as an accounts clerk with British Rail's accounts head office in London. H decided to pursue her first degree at the Open University whilst working in the first of these posts. H pursued a course in social science, followed by postgraduate qualifications in education, as well as an Advanced Academic Diploma. With a passion similar to L's for minority ethnic youth issues, she followed these activities with a trainer's certificate in careers education and guidance; finally achieving her Master's degree in vocational education and guidance.

Where H is concerned, however, there was quite a gap between her original postgraduate activities and the acquisition of her Master's degree, since her instinctive desire to ensure that she utilized her skills in the most appropriate manner on behalf of disadvantaged youth from minority ethnic communities, meant that her period of working took her through a series of posts, from schools at secondary level, through to lecturing at FE college level; various posts as head of careers departments; and the deputy directorship of a sixth form centre.

Interestingly, all these posts were in Inner London Boroughs with high density minority ethnic populations, with a heavy emphasis on equal opportunities strategies, including multilingual counselling. With the new approach to Access courses and return-to-learning courses for adults, H chose also to specialize in these areas.

Unlike L, who had no children of her own, H has two extremely academically able girls, both of whom, under the guidance of herself and a very supportive husband, have achieved at the highest level. The older of the two has already had two careers, first as a chartered accountant and now as a barrister. She has, in a sense, followed in her mother's footsteps by giving something back to society through working in a law centre in a deprived area of London. The second daughter is a specialist computer systems manager for a large company. Parental involvement and awareness of 'the game' as far as the education of minority ethnic young people is concerned, quite obviously had an impact on the success of both girls.

H has now taken early retirement in order to fulfil her desire to become an educational consultant; her disillusionment with the lack of progress made by so many young Afro-Caribbean students in inner city areas has prompted this decision. She feels that being freed from the bureaucracy involved in the day-to-day functioning of a local education authority would allow her to work in the way she prefers.

J

J's decision to go into the field of education, whilst stemming from a no less passionate concern to ensure that pupils from minority ethnic backgrounds were given an opportunity to achieve their full potential, began its course from a slightly different perspective.

J, unlike L and H, completed her secondary education in the UK, at a top independent girls' school, to which she had been sent by her parents so that she could achieve her potential in the creative and performing arts, on a part-time basis, at one of the large music conservatoires, whilst completing her 'A' levels. J was born in Trinidad, but by the age of 14 had literally outgrown all that Trinidad had to offer to her in the field of classical music.

After being awarded places to both university to read history and psychology, as well as to another of London's top music conservatoires, J opted to take up the place at the music conservatoire, where she remained for five years, gaining both her first degree and a number of postgraduate music qualifications. However, when considering whether to take up a scholarship to further her musical studies in Europe, J discovered that her true vocation lay in teaching and in education.

Within two months J had found a post teaching music in a comprehensive girls' school in one of Inner London's most cosmopolitan and deprived boroughs, becoming head of the lower school department three months after her arrival. Her administrative skills were further recognized when, three years later, she was promoted to head of a large music department in a mixed comprehensive school.

What happened next is indicative of the many obstacles faced by Afro-Caribbean teaching staff in the late 1960s and early 1970s. Having raised the reputation of the performing arts in the school, and, indeed, in the then Inner London Education Authority, J had noted, along the way, a distinct difference not only in the treatment of minority ethnic pupils, but in the education of girls. J approached the necessary authority for permission to be seconded, in order to return to university to research the whole area of curriculum studies. She was told, however, that she would be difficult to replace, and her application was refused. In the meanwhile, J noted that the application of other 'less successful' teachers for secondment was being granted.

In the end, after two years of rejected applications for secondment, J resigned her post to return to her own full-time education, a decision which she has never regretted. Following the acquisition of her Advanced Academic Diploma in the theory and practice of curriculum studies, J went on to become one of the few black Afro-Caribbean women, at that time, to achieve her Master's degree in curriculum planning and design. Amongst the numerous activities in which she became involved soon after completion of this degree was lecturing to postgraduate students in two universities in South East England on the impact of multi-cultural education across the curriculum in secondary education.

J's third child was born immediately following the award of this degree, prompting her to work on a part-time basis at two totally different independent girls' schools. As a black woman in the world of work at this level, and because of the incremental and cumulative nature of promotion in education, the onus was on the individual to stay in the mainstream at all costs. The advantage was, of course, that one was then able to guide one's own offspring through the maze of educational theories which were being bandied about at that time. As such J's own children have all excelled at school.

J went on to achieve success as a chief officer and an assistant director of education for the post-schools division in a large Inner London cosmopolitan borough, following a period of work in the voluntary sector, primarily to assist decision-makers, whose work impacted on students of Afro-Caribbean origin, to come to the right conclusions when faced with issues specifically thrown up by these young people. She coordinated courses in West Indian sociology for magistrates, probation officers, educational psychologists, teachers, lecturers, social workers and, of course, parents, at the same time as managing the DHSS's only Afro-Caribbean intermediate treatment centre. J is now not only on the list of advisers to the Secretary of State for Education, but also a non-executive director in one of London's largest health commissioning agencies. Because of this and her interest in ensuring that other members of minority ethnic groups receive information pertinent to public service appointments, J has become a 'mentor' to the Cabinet Office's public appointment unit, with specific reference to assisting new recruits in this area.

Like H above, J is seeking to establish her own management and research consultancy, free from the constraints of local education authority bureaucracy. Her concerns are very similar: to ensure that the correct information is disseminated to those who need it most at the optimum time in their career progression.

Conclusion

The career paths of these individuals can be said to be fairly representative of those who, after achieving the necessary initial degree/HE qualification, and where appropriate a Post Graduate Certificate in Education, have made an informed decision to remain in the field of higher education.

When one attempts to make any type of comparison with their indigenous peers, the career paths of the latter tend, more often than not, to be far more subject-specific, e.g. in disciplines such as geography, modern languages, physical sciences, etc. Today, black Afro-Caribbean women who have completed their tertiary education in such discrete disciplines invariably choose not to work in education *per se*. Given the wider choices now available to them, and advances in new technology in a variety of consumer-oriented fields, many younger black women now tend to merge imperceptibly into careers formerly considered to be the domain of individuals other than themselves.

Without wishing to make sweeping generalizations or in any way whatever seeking to diminish their achievements, one needs to recognize that what makes the younger generation so obviously different from their female forebears is the fact that the latter, in the particular historical period to which I refer, found themselves in circumstances which required a response to the needs of their community. It was almost as if the decision to be a career educationist had been made for them; that for the most part, having qualifications in the social sciences, there was an urgency to be both reactive and proactive; the need to disseminate their newly found discoveries about the lack of attention paid to personal issues as they related to minority ethnic communities, led them into research or into direct interaction at the institutional level with students and staff alike.

This natural progression from imparting information to others within the same profession, to the more public service-oriented areas, remains firmly rooted in their psyche and, of course, in their personal work profiles, as well as in the expectations of their indigenous counterparts who are as yet unable to resolve fully the issues which they continue to highlight for the benefit of society as a whole.

7

UK Women at the Very Top: An American Assessment

Karen Doyle Walton

I served concurrently as a Fulbright Administrative Fellow at La Sainte Union College of Higher Education in Southampton and as a Visiting Scholar at Wolfson College, Cambridge University. Although the areas of my Fulbright research were faculty and staff assessment, long-range planning, academic administrative structures, and student and faculty foreign exchange programmes, the sabbatical leave also provided an excellent opportunity to study the women who have reached the highest rung of the British higher education ladder. The research consisted of interviewing a range of women who held or recently held vice-chancellorships or Oxbridge college headships.

Keenly aware of the culture differences between the US and the UK, the first question that arose was, 'Are these women "at the very top" accessible to a female academician from America?' and if so, 'How does one gain "an audience" to ask personal, somewhat intrusive questions of these leaders?' Finally, 'Would they answer the questions?' and, 'What would be their demeanour in offering or denying forthright responses?' I was not optimistic about the reception I would receive, perhaps because of American stereotypes of the British as formal and distant. For the 11 women included in this study, that stereotype could not be further from the truth.

Entrance to the inner sanctums

A simple telephone call to the secretary or personal assistant of the 11 heads of colleges, followed by a letter of introduction from the UK Fulbright Commission, a brief letter explaining the nature of the study, and a copy of my *curriculum vitae* yielded a one-hour (or longer) interview, usually within one week of my request. In almost every case, I was offered a hospitable cup of tea and biscuits, lunch, or a glass of sherry, depending on the time of day or evening. The setting for each interview was the principal's office, with the exception of the apartment of the one retired interviewee and the lobby of the Savoy Hotel for a principal who was a Women of the Year Luncheon honoree at that venue. (Heads of Oxbridge colleges hold various titles such as principal, president and mistress. For convenience, they are referred to as principal here.)

Their private offices were usually spacious suites with a large conference table and chairs, a functional desk in a working corner, and a comfortable sofa and chairs in a conversational area. Several of the principals' offices were warmed by a friendly fire and book-lined walls, and almost all were furnished with graciously-worn antiques or reproductions.

Institutional profiles

The women interviewed head very different institutions in that those at Oxford and Cambridge colleges manage establishments having enrolments of some 400 students on average, with the smallest being not much over 100 and the largest over 600. The heads of British universities, however, manage bodies with 15–20,000 students with corresponding multi-million pound budgets. Yet despite the disparity in institutional size, the parallels in the nature of the jobs are sufficiently close to warrant comparisons and, viewed from an American perspective, the status of the women is not dissimilar. Indeed, it is interesting to note that one vice-chancellor of a British university has now taken the position of head of a Cambridge women's college.

In the United States, the American Council on Education's Office of Women in Higher Education (OWHE) conducted a study of women college and university presidents who were in office in December 1985. The survey instrument was completed by 88 per cent of all women presidents of institutions accredited by one of the six regional accrediting bodies. The majority of the four-year public institutions with female presidents had full-time-equivalents (FTE) of more than 5,000 students, and only 4 per cent of those institutions had enrolments fewer than 500. Twenty-two per cent of the four-year independent institutions with women presidents had enrolments fewer than 500, 43 per cent had enrolments of 501 to 1,000, and only four per cent had enrolments over 3,000 (Touchton *et al.*, 1993).

Admittedly the colleges in Oxford and Cambridge are institutionally quite different from colleges in the United States. As one principal explained it,

> Oxbridge colleges are elements of a large university, with major research ambitions in every field. The colleges provide an institutional structure that is orthogonal to university structures, and which delivers a range of academic and ancillary services, but by no means a full range. In particular, the students at these colleges obtain their degrees from the university, are examined by the university, and must meet university standards in all respects.

The American institutions, on the other hand, are more 'self-contained', providing a complete range of services and granting their own degrees.

Personal profiles

Biographical information on ten of the British principals was found in *Who's Who*, which revealed that their average age was 57 years and their median age was 59 (excluding the one retired principal). In the OWHE survey of American women presidents, both the mean and median ages of four-year public and independent institutions fell in the range of 50 to 54, making the American comparison group slightly younger than the British principals included in this study (Touchton *et al.*, 1993).

The average number of years the British principals had held their present offices was four, and the median was three (again excluding the retiree). Although they were not asked their marital status, seven mentioned they were married (one of whom also stated she was divorced), four referred to their children (numbering from one to four) and one alluded to four grand-children.

In contrast, an article in the *THES* entitled 'Women's circuitous routes to the top' described four American female presidents of prestigious colleges and universities: Hannah Gray, the retired president of the University of Chicago; Donna Shalala, former chancellor of the University of Wisconsin and Secretary of Health and Human Resources under President Bill Clinton; Nannerl Keohane, former President of Wellesley College (a prestigious women's college), appointed President of Duke University in 1993; and Diana Natalicio, President of the University of Texas at El Paso. The article states that American women 'have made progress and now make up twelve per cent of the higher education chief executives at the 3,000 institutions, but the advance has been slow – and certainly slower at private colleges.' Hodges (1992) ends the article by saying, 'What sets all these women apart from the majority of their sisters is that none of them had children. The real test is whether women with families will find it possible to progress in the same way.'

The OWHE survey of women presidents found that 26 per cent of respondents from four-year public institutions were never married, 44 per cent were married, and 26 per cent were separated or divorced. The comparable figures for women presidents of four-year independent institutions were 67 per cent never married, 20 per cent were married, and 8 per cent were separated or divorced (Touchton *et al.*, 1993).

Educational backgrounds

Ten of the 11 British women principals received bachelor's and master's degrees from present or former women's colleges of Cambridge or Oxford (two each from Girton in Cambridge and St Anne's, Lady Margaret Hall, and Somerville in Oxford, and one each from New Hall, Cambridge, and St Hilda's, Oxford). Five had earned doctorates from Oxford (in chemistry and in history), Cambridge (in archaeology), Harvard (in philosophy), and

King's College, London (in English). In addition, one principal had received a BA from Barnard College (the women's college of Columbia University) before completing her BA at Oxford; and another had earned an MA from Brandeis University in Massachusetts as well as an MA from Oxford. Two women referred to their pre-college years at King Edward VI High School for Girls, Edgbaston, two attended Christ's Hospital, Hertford (an 'old fashioned girls' boarding school'), and three mentioned other girls' schools.

In the American survey, 22 per cent of the women presidents of public institutions and 63 per cent from independent institutions had earned their baccalaureate degrees from women's colleges. All of the American women presidents of public institutions had earned doctorates. Seventy-seven per cent of the women presidents of independent institutions had earned PhD or EdD degrees, and an additional 4 per cent held other professional degrees beyond their master's (Touchton *et al.*, 1993).

Academic career paths

The five principals with earned doctorates, a sixth with a master's degree, and a seventh whose speciality is law have taught in colleges and universities. One finished her doctorate from King's College in 18 months, became a permanent lecturer at the age of 23, taught for 23 years, and then held various academic administrative positions (e.g., registrar for arts and humanities at the Council for National Academic Awards and deputy rector, academic, of a polytechnic) before becoming a vice-chancellor. This principal published more books and articles after the birth of her only child than before.

An archaeologist rose through the administrative positions of admissions tutor, member of the Council of Senate, head of department, and member of the finance and building committees of a university while teaching. She was the only principal who mentioned that she still teaches a lecture course in her college and a course for the university, while authoring a book between her first and second years as principal.

In addition to teaching at colleges and universities in the UK, one principal has served as a Visiting Scholar at Yale University and at Bryn Mawr College (which, with Barnard and Wellesley, was one of the selective 'Seven Sister Colleges'). She founded the *London Journal*, acted as its editor-in-chief, and was literary director of the Royal Historical Society and the first female editor of their publication.

The Harvard PhD philosopher taught both at Barnard College (leaving a tenured position at the rank of associate professor) and at the University of Essex. The Oxford chemist taught at several colleges and universities, held administrative positions, belonged to university committees, and founded New Hall College, Cambridge. The only interviewee who had been called to the bar (Inner Temple) had taught law both in Canada and at Oxford, where she also held administrative posts and committee memberships. A principal who 'took off 11 years' to have her children wrote three books during that time and taught at high school and university levels in the United States, Canada and England before and after her child-rearing period.

Almost all of these seven principals who reached their top positions by following the academic career path of teaching, administrative positions, and committee memberships had also published articles and books.

In comparison, 96 per cent of the women presidents of American public institutions who responded to the OWHE survey held one of the following positions immediately before holding their current presidencies: executive vice-president (7 per cent), assistant to the president (4 per cent), vice-president for academic affairs (33 per cent), associate or assistant vice-president for academic affairs (4 per cent), academic dean (30 per cent), other vice-presidencies (4 per cent), and other presidencies (15 per cent). Women presidents of American independent colleges and universities who responded to the OWHE survey held similar positions immediately before holding their current presidencies, e.g., 53 per cent held administrative positions in academic affairs, and 4 per cent held other college or university presidencies. However, unlike their sister presidents of public institutions, 10 per cent of the women presidents of independent institutions held administrative positions in student affairs, 13 per cent held faculty positions immediately preceding their presidencies, 4 per cent were K-12 administrators, 6 per cent held religious positions, and 8 per cent held neither educational nor religious positions immediately preceding their presidencies (Touchton *et al.*, 1993).

Foreign service

The second most common career path of the 11 female principals was foreign service. After attaining increasingly more responsible and influential positions in NATO, in the diplomatic service, and at the United Nations, one of the interviewees became the first woman ever to serve as a British ambassador. During her seven-year tenure as Ambassador to Denmark, the small size of the country allowed her to know leaders from all walks of life. She modestly attributes her appointment to that position to 'being in the right place at the right time.' However, unlike the American granting of ambassadorships as 'political plums,' British appointments to foreign countries are civil service positions based on competence and experience. The fact that I briefly crossed paths with the former ambassador in the courtyard of a Cambridge college several days after our interview and the ambassador referred to me by name was evidence of the fact that her diplomatic talents remained keen.

A second interviewee had served as ambassador to Luxembourg for three and a half years after holding diplomatic positions in places such as The Hague, Bangkok and Paris and dealing in such diverse fields as the European Community and South East Asian affairs. Both women alluded to the fact that, before 1972, any woman who married automatically lost her foreign service post; however, men were not required to relinquish their positions unless they married a foreigner. A third principal who spent part of her career in Her Majesty's Diplomatic Service had worked in East Europe, Bangkok, Paris and Bonn, where she supervised approximately one-half of the embassy. Although diplomatic service has the lure of intrigue, before the war one needed private resources to take most diplomatic posts, because they paid so little.

Government experience

Two women previously held various government positions. In one case such appointments included the Under Secretary in the Department of Trade, Deputy Secretary of the Department of Trade and Industry, and UK Director of the European Investment Bank.

In addition to her substantial career in education, one principal is a member of the House of Lords, and a second solid academician served the war effort as a Chief Officer (a rank) in the Women's Royal Naval Service (WRNS) from 1942 to 1946. During the war, 40 chief officers were in charge of approximately 100,000 WRNS.

Presidential search process

The common procedure for recruiting a British college principal is for the governing fellows of the college to develop a pool of candidates through such means as searching in *Who's Who*, headhunters, networking, accepting nominations from friends and colleagues of candidates, and accepting self-nominations from candidates. Some replied to public advertisement of the post. Several women believed that their heightened visibility through university committee work, foreign service, and other government posts had enhanced their likelihood of being nominated or being asked to apply for the position of principal. Two women had been internal candidates.

One principal described the interview process for her presidency as a two and a half hour session with the college's governing body during which her work and educational policy with respect to Cambridge were discussed. Her appointment required a two-thirds vote of the fellows.

Two others had previously been headhunted for headships of Oxbridge colleges, but declined because one was involved with the preparations for a government White Paper and the other withdrew at an early stage, because she felt that her 'fit' with the interested college was not good.

One principal has found it to be burdensome to deal with an unsuccessful internal candidate and her supporters who have remained on the staff. Another said that while she had no trouble getting 'short listed' for principal offices, she had been unsuccessful at landing the job. However, her interviewing skills improved with practice, leading to her present position.

More than one interviewee knew that her college had specifically sought a female principal. (Some of these institutions are required by statute to do so.) Another had been headhunted by several American colleges, but felt that in those searches she was merely being used as an affirmative action figure rather than a serious candidate. It is her opinion that affirmative action demeans women in the United States and that Cambridge does not operate under an affirmative action policy.

One vice-chancellor survived four days of interviews, knowing that she was the only woman on a short list of seven candidates. 'It was a challenge to stay through the round of interviews, and an even greater challenge to take up the job when it was offered' (Ozga, 1993).

The American counterparts who were internal candidates for the position of president comprised 51 per cent of the respondents to the OWHE survey from independent colleges and universities and 26 per cent from public institutions. Fewer than 8 per cent were contacted by a search firm, and the majority of the women presidents had been nominated for their positions (Touchton *et al.*, 1993).

Parental or other family influence

The family backgrounds of the British principals varied greatly, but in most cases they received encouragement and support from their parents and husbands (where applicable). One principal described her childhood as 'oddish', since the family followed her father on his army assignments in far-away places such as South Africa and Palestine. Her enrolment in several schools necessitated by his career advancement made her self-reliant and adaptable.

One of the many principals who attended a girls' boarding school as a teenager found that she learned to do things for herself under those circumstances. Another stated that no woman in her family had previously had a career although, like several other principals, her mother had attended a university.

One principal traced her initiative and indefatigability back to her great-grandmother, the widow of a well-to-do ship's captain from Sunderland who was killed at sea. This industrious woman took in washing to support 11 children and to pay a penny a week for the principal's grandmother to attend the local dameschool. The grandmother appreciated her mother's financial sacrifice and completed her studies one year early, at the age of 11, to lessen the monetary outlay. The principal's mother attended the London College of Music and determined that her daughter would matriculate in college. She also received encouragement from her father, the president of a theological college, who gave his 7-year-old daughter books by Jeans-Jacques Rousseau and John Stuart Mill, which she gladly read.

Another principal was 12 years old when World War II broke out, causing her relocation into the United States with her American mother. After attending high school and college in the States, with her father's encouragement, she entered the British diplomatic service.

One principal, the daughter of an engineer and Member of Parliament, resigned her university professorship on being elected to her present post.

The father of the chemist vice-chancellor and head of college had been in the navy. She was always interested in science, but the science teaching at the girls' boarding school she attended in her youth was poor, as it was at similar institutions. She was the eldest of three girls and three boys, and was as likely to receive a Meccano set for Christmas as a doll.

Other encouragement received

Two principals identified other women in higher education administration who had functioned as mentors during their rise to the top. One mentor was, in fact, the retired vice-chancellor and head of college interviewed as part of this research project. One principal has been 'pushed along by men on top levels of authority,' and another was encouraged while employed in the civil service, 'one of the earliest equal opportunity organizations in England.' This sentiment is echoed by Baroness Pauline Perry, former Vice-Chancellor of South Bank University, in Jenny Ozga's book, *Women in Educational Management* (1993):

> Although the civil-service statistics show that it is still not easy for women
> to reach the higher ranks, nevertheless I think there would be few
> women in the senior ranks of the civil service who would claim any preju-
> dice or handicap. By its tradition, the civil service rewards those who
> deliver, who communicate well and who work collaboratively rather than
> competitively with their colleagues.

One former diplomat felt that being a woman has sometimes been an asset to the performance of her duties. For example, while a junior representative at the United Nations, she was readily identifiable and could more easily disregard hierarchy in striking up discussion with most male senior delegates because of her gender.

Discouraging factors

In contrast, one principal stated that backlashes are powerful in England and warned that prejudices with regard to gender and class cannot be underestimated. They necessitate careful manoeuvering to avoid or minimize them.

An experienced principal recalled that when she was chair of the history department at another university, male colleagues would sometimes say, 'If Dr [her name] were not here, I could tell you very simply. . . .'

One principal of a women's college feels that most women who have made it have had to be 'honorary men.' She observed that in order for a woman

to reach the highest levels in the civil service and concurrently be a successful mother and wife, she would have to have a 'perfect nanny and house-
keeper.' In academic positions, the percentage of female professors is very
low; and there is a preponderance of men in staff positions, except in areas
consisting of 'women's work.'

Another principal of a women's college who is divorced also said that combining children and career is very difficult. She noted the small percentage
of female professors and felt that the retrenchment in British universities in
the 1980s reduced the number of entry-level jobs in higher education at a
time when more women were receiving PhDs. Her friends have been pleased
with her appointment to the position of principal, and she has not experienced a 'glass ceiling'. On the contrary, she stated that, 'I get appointed to
significant university committees. I expect to be taken seriously on committees, and I am.'

In contrast, a different principal remarked that, 'Some women think that
if another woman has "made it," by definition she has betrayed her "sisters".'
She has not been appointed to male-dominated committees such as build-
ings or finances, despite her seniority within the university. Not being taken
seriously by some top-level men has resulted in her placement on committees usually regarded as female-oriented. She opined that many women
prefer to be academicians rather than administrators. The expectation of
frequent publication means that fewer women are promoted to the rank of
professor, in part due to their family obligations and the fact that women
appear to be provided with fewer resources such as computers and secretarial
help.

A completely different view is held by yet another principal of a women's
college who said it never occurred to her that being a woman wasn't an
advantage.

When Baroness Perry was promoted to Staff Inspector in Her Majesty's
Inspectorate, her first chief inspector warned her that she should anticipate
two kinds of reactions from her former colleagues: 'Those who were your
friends but who now no longer wish to be so; those who were not your friends
before but who now suddenly seek to become so. It is a judge of your character which you find the more painful.' Baroness Perry thinks that it is 'more
painful for a woman than for a man – to find that one is no longer "one of
the gang" but in a senior position.' She and other women colleagues in
management positions have found it particularly difficult during the first
year of a senior position to deal with men and women 'who would use my
perceived female vulnerability to try to win sympathy for their own inadequacy: "You will understand, Pauline, I am having problems with my health"
or ". . . at home" ' (Ozga, 1993).

In a November 6 1992 issue of the *THES*, Baroness Perry referred to professorships as the 'natural breeding ground for the post of vice-chancellor.'
She lamented that since less than 4 per cent of UK professors were women,
senior positions in colleges and universities attracted very few female applicants. Perry characterized the world of higher education as a 'male club' and

asserted that, 'For a woman to pull out of a crowd and to move up the ladder of management responsibility is extremely difficult.'

In addition to the percentage of female professors in the UK being low, a survey conducted by the Association of University Teachers (AUT) found that female professors earn £2,000 per annum less than their male counterparts. Whereas this salary discrepancy had previously been attributed to the fact that more women teach in the 'soft disciplines' which pay lower salaries, the AUT survey found that female professors fared badly in all areas. Alison Utley wrote in a 30 August 1991 *THES* article entitled, 'Women profess to salary bias' that, 'More than half of all women professors (53 per cent) earned less than £30,000 while the figure for men was 28 per cent.' Hence from a financial standpoint, professorships are not particularly alluring 'natural breeding grounds' for nurturing women who aspire to the position of principal of colleges and universities.

In a 1990 *THES* article entitled, 'Outlook bleak for female factor,' Karen MacGregor reports the results of a survey of ten polytechnics conducted by Jean Bocock, Assistant Secretary for Higher Education at the National Association of Teachers in Further and Higher Education, and Mollie Temple, Head of Access Development at Leeds Polytechnic (now Metropolitan University). They found that women accounted for 33 per cent of the researchers at those polytechnics, 49 per cent of the lecturers, and 36 per cent of senior lecturers. However, on the higher levels, only 15 per cent of principal lecturers/readers were women, 12 per cent of heads of department, and 13 per cent of senior managers (defined to be 'members of directorates or deans of faculty') were female. Bocock and Temple stated that, 'The pool from which the next generation of women managers will be recruited is not large enough to ensure that the proportion of women in higher grades will increase in the near future unless very positive steps are taken to ensure change.' Their report concludes that, 'Commitments to equal opportunity are very much intentional rather than reality.'

Sian Griffiths' *THES* article of 5 October 1991, entitled 'Britain backward on sex bias,' described an international comparative study on women in university education conducted by Jennifer Johnson at Robinson College, Cambridge. Griffiths concluded that, 'British universities are in the "farcical" situation of calling themselves equal opportunities employers without the machinery or statistics to back this up. . . .' However, the woman principal of a Cambridge college I interviewed made the point that her college is 'exclusively single sex in membership, including teaching and research fellowships.'

In the *Fact Book on Women in Higher Education,* Judith Touchton, Deputy Director of OWHE, and Lynne Davis (1991) report that in 1984, 45 per cent of the men teaching at American four-year colleges and universities held the rank of full professor, while only 16 per cent of women teaching in higher education held that rank. In the same year, one-half of the women faculty members at four-year institutions held doctoral degrees, compared with 70 per cent of the men. Hence on both sides of the Atlantic the pools which spawn university principals are overstocked with males.

A later AUT study reported by Alison Utley in a 27 December 1991 *THES* article entitled 'Women lose out of jobs' revealed that:

> . . . overall, 88 per cent of women were paid on lecturer scales compared to just 63 per cent of males. Ten per cent of women were senior lecturers compared to a quarter of male academics. Only 2 per cent of women were professors compared to 12 per cent of males.

Within each grade, women's salaries were also lower than men's. Female lecturers earned 92 per cent of the men's pay, and 94 per cent of men's salaries in the rank of professor. AUT researcher Tom Wilson stated that, 'It is clear that women are not getting promoted. Research is the key criterion for promotion and arguably men have more time and are in a better position to engage in such activity' (Utley, 1991b).

Utley reported that 'many heads of institutions are uncomfortable with the disproportionate number of women holding senior academic posts. There is also growing concern over the male dominance of vice-chancellorships.' In response, most institutions have adopted a code of practice for equal opportunities issued in 1990 by the Committee of Vice Chancellors and Principals. The code recommended that each institution include in an annual report information concerning the gender of applicants, interviewees, new appointments, promotions, and discretionary award recipients. Although most institutions have complied with the recommendation, the code has been criticized as being too soft (Utley, 1991b).

In the United States, 89 per cent of the women presidents who responded to the OWHE questionnaire believed it to be important or very important to review their institutions' policies to eliminate gender bias; 83 per cent thought that all searches should be required to yield a significant number of women candidates; and 64 per cent felt that gender equity should be part of the reward system for faculty and administrators. However, only 35 per cent of the respondents believed it important to publish an annual report on the progress of women in their institutions with respect to those issues (Touchton *et al.*, 1991).

Leadership styles

Several British principals acknowledged their ability to get people to work as a team rather than 'throw one's weight around and lay down the law to get things done.' Two stated that, because colleges are democratic, the top position has no power but much influence. Another 'loves committee work,' and through her skill in making speeches can explain ideas and gain support for her initiatives.

The research skills of one principal were particularly obvious when, during the interview, she alluded to two relevant documents, which she promptly located in her files, and to factual information she retrieved from her computer. In the offices of the other women, no computers were in view.

One recently appointed principal who prefers managing by democratic consensus related that, when appropriate and necessary, she takes a strong initiative and assumes a conventional, strict leadership style.

Foreign service gave one principal the opportunity to observe others' leadership styles and to develop her own. She acknowledged that the lack of power of an Oxbridge head of college position frustrates some colleagues with backgrounds in business or industry.

Another principal regards her job as very political, requiring lateral thinking and discussion. She admitted that it takes time to become accustomed to this *modus operandi,* and one must learn not to 'lose face if you don't get what you want.'

One of the former diplomats learned at Whitehall how to encourage collaborative work, leading to 'harmony, like a choir.' One principal views herself as a strong manager and 'a shaker,' but likens running a university to running a family and views herself as a 'soft touch.'

Although another principal has had experience on university-wide committees, she credits her archaeological research skills and field experiences for her administrative and management successes, which have required her to organize people in order to complete projects.

One principal believes that parenting ('the experience of creating a home and a loving family team') develops one's leadership capabilities and is 'increasingly one which is in tune with the styles of management appropriate for the 1990s.' She referred to rejecting 'the old macho management styles of the past generation' and replacing them with 'creativity, communication, vision, symbolism and even love' as characteristics of good, modern management. Many women are well-suited for leadership roles which are enhanced by good communication skills, 'antennae for the feelings and moods of those around them, . . . a climate in which people feel that they are trusted,' and 'a sense of mutual trust and tolerance that is felt within the best families, where individuals know they may make mistakes and be forgiven, because they share a common set of goals and values' (Ozga, 1993).

The introduction to *Women in Educational Management* (Ozga, 1993) is entitled, 'In a Different Mode.' In it, Jenny Ozga states that '. . . the opportunity will have been missed if women's increased presence in educational management makes no difference to management practice, if women are simply absorbed into management and become indistinguishable from men.' She turns her attention away from 'strategies for change which encouraged women to adopt masculine behaviours and values – to be competitive, aggressive; to look like men – as evidenced in their crassest form in the wave of 1980s advertising, films and pulp fiction featuring power-dressed women executives.'

Observers of American females 'at the top' in the 1980s could find not only 'power-dressed women executives' in the boardrooms of industry, but also on the highest rungs of college and university administration. I do not know whether women in those positions in Britain 'dressed for success' in the 1980s by 'aping' men but, after interviewing the 11 women in this study, it is difficult to imagine that they succumbed to such outward manifestations of insecurity.

A 'managerial class' in higher education administration

In 1991 and 1993, The Pew Charitable Trusts sponsored three international round-table discussions at which 24 'university citizens' from 12 countries on both sides of the Atlantic assessed the challenges and opportunities now facing universities. Two members of the transatlantic dialogue were Robert Atwell and Madeleine Green, President and Vice President, respectively, of the American Council on Education. Their thoughts concerning the round-table discussions were expressed in an article entitled, 'A view from the United States: forces for change' (Green and Atwell, 1993). They believe that US educational institutions are less resistant to reform because of a 'managerial class of presidents, vice-presidents, and deans, who see themselves not as professors briefly dabbling in administration but as executives engaged in academic enterprises. . . .' They believe that the continental European process of electing rectors by professors and students and of empowering faculty senates makes reform difficult. US presidents have little direct power, but they have more leverage than their European counterparts through budgetary authority, executive powers delegated to them by their boards of trustees, and connections with external constituencies.

The retired vice-chancellor/head of a Cambridge college does not consider being principal of a college to be an eminent profession of a British man or woman. She feels that academic administration is not a career, and that academicians regard a professorship as the ultimate goal. Head of college is a post one assumes after having held other career posts. This opinion is illustrated by one of the interviewees who announced her retirement as head of college effective at the end of the academic year, marking the end of her third successful career at the age of 67.

Job satisfaction and stress

While in office, the former Vice-Chancellor/head of college was tired, but not worried. Most Sundays were reserved for relaxation through gardening and bookbinding, which allowed her to combine the aesthetic with the practical, working with her hands. The fact that she always lived in college and never married made it easier to fulfil the numerous responsibilities of her position.

A newly appointed principal admitted that the position involves periodic stress, but so does being a professor. She has not felt isolated and has remained primarily an academician, staying current in her field on the international level.

In contrast, another principal mentioned that the 'experience of isolation is a part of the role of the head of any institution.' In a *THES* article entitled, 'Prospects poor for women,' Baroness Perry relates the following story:

> I have never forgotten one woman head of a school commenting on how lonely she felt on her job, and saying to me: 'The worst experience of a head is to walk along the corridor and hear the laughter coming from the staff room, knowing that if you enter the room it would stop'.
>
> (Perry, 1992)

When asked whether she likes her job, one experienced principal smiled immediately and said that she found observing the development of undergraduate students to be very fulfilling. Another principal has found her present job less stressful than previous ones. She has learned to manage stress and is happier than ever before.

In general, each of the interviewees seemed very happy in their present jobs and felt that the rigours of their positions were more than compensated by the satisfaction they received. Baroness Perry expressed this view in the *THES* in the following way:

> The compensations and pleasures of course are infinite. Running any institution is a creative experience, but this is most of all true for a university, with its rich community of students of many ages; academic staff whose creativity and dedication to their job is probably nowhere exceeded in industry, and the inspiration of a job which extends the boundaries of achievement for so many young people.

Similar job satisfaction was expressed by American college and university presidents in the OWHE's 1985 survey. Ninety-nine per cent of the respondents were satisfied or highly satisfied with their jobs. Seventy per cent of women presidents of public, four-year institutions believed that they were doing a good job as did 62 per cent of respondents from private institutions (Touchton *et al.*, 1991).

Encouragement of other women

The retired vice-chancellor of Cambridge has never considered herself a feminist, but she has always encouraged other women to 'do whatever they wanted.' The principal of a Cambridge college who regards the former vice-chancellor as her mentor supports an extensive professional development programme for her own faculty. Younger faculty who are experienced in current research and publication techniques give seminars to older faculty who wish to update their skills. She encourages women to serve on committees and pursue academic administration, acknowledging a women's network within the university that assists female colleagues in obtaining desired committee memberships.

A *THES* article of 27 December 1991 describes Vice-Chancellor Anne Wright's commitment to promoting equal opportunities at Sunderland

University. After commissioning an audit of the percentages of women, ethnic minorities and disabled students and staff, Dr Wright took steps to improve Sunderland statistics, which she admits were in some cases worse than national averages. From 1989 to 1991, the percentage of women lecturers at Sunderland increased from 17.8 per cent to 19.5 per cent. (The national average is 22.9 per cent.) During the same period, female principal lecturers rose from 7 to 10 per cent, and female senior lecturers increased from 15 to 17 per cent. Significant increases were also realized in the percentage of women in administrative staff positions. In particular, the percentage of female principal officers jumped from 18.5 per cent to 33.5 per cent and senior officers from 57 to 69 per cent. Dr Wright has established training programmes which include fair recruitment procedures, image and self-projection for women, and assertiveness (rather than aggressiveness) for men (Griffiths, 1991b).

Baroness Perry states that, 'Perhaps the best aspect of the situation lies in one's ability to help other women up the steep-sided pyramid.' She remains 'convinced that networks are an essential support for women as they move into posts where responsibilities and painful isolation undermine their confidence.' Perry warns against becoming exclusionary, but advises instead that, 'Both the world of work and the world of home are better when they are shared in equal partnership by men and women together, rather than when either tries to exclude the other.' The response to 'all-male clubs, the all-male organizations, the old-boys' networks should not be to set up

> all-female clubs and missions. Many women (though not all) have great talents in healing relationships and in creating new bridges: their involvement in public life and in the market-place should surely mean that sexism can be conquered and that the human race can acknowledge the spread of its many talents through male and female alike.
>
> (Ozga, 1993)

Salaries

Salaries were not discussed in these interviews, except in one case when a principal mentioned that she worked at her job full-time, although it was notionally a half-time position. She casually stated that the pension from her previous career enabled her to take this job which paid little, but was challenging and enjoyable. It was obvious that her dedication to the college was sincere, and that financial remuneration was not a consideration. Salary statistics for Oxford colleges and the two universities included in this study were not readily available, but those for Cambridge were listed in the *Cambridge University Reporter*. It is noteworthy that the 31 Cambridge colleges range in size from Trinity College with total enrolment of some 1,000 full- and part-time students in 1993–94, to one with a total enrolment of under 150 full- and part-time students at the college headed by the principal under discussion. An examination of the salaries of the other female heads of Cambridge colleges indicates that the females' salaries are comparable to their male counterparts. Specifically, the 1993–94 salary of the head of Trinity College was £61,437, and the 1993–94 salary of the largest Cambridge college headed by a woman was £47,556, according to the *Cambridge University Reporter* of 16 March 1995. Virtually all the male and female heads of colleges were earning, at this date, a salary of £40–50,000. That source does not state what, if any, perquisites (such as housing, food, travel and entertainment budgets, and maid service) are provided to the heads of the various colleges in addition to their base salaries.

The 1993–94 financial year was the first one in which information relating to the pay of vice-chancellors and principals became available. Of the over 80 English higher education institutions which published figures, 28 disclosed packages worth more than £100,000 and a further 15 of £90,000 or more. The figures must be treated with care, as some give details of pay, pensions and benefits, while others declare only a salary figure. From 1994–95, all institutions had to disclose information. The pay for women heads of institutions does not appear out of line with pay for male heads of comparable institutions, ranging from £70,000 upwards, with the women heads, none of whom leads the largest or most prestigious institutions, attracting salaries within the £80–£90,000 range.

Fundraising

Two women principals related that, in the past, the position of head of college was often held by distinguished academics. However, with the increasing importance of fundraising, colleges are recruiting heads with the experience or potential to cultivate donors.

An Oxford principal in office for two years estimated that she spent approximately half of her time in fundraising activities. Her college had recently completed a new student residence costing approximately £1.2 million for which they received no government grants. A second Oxford principal stated that all the colleges must raise funds, requiring the head's attention which previously would have been focused on the undergraduates. She estimated that fundraising activities accounted for 20 to 25 per cent of her time.

The former Cambridge vice-chancellor and head of college recalled that when she was vice-chancellor from 1975 to 1977 that post required no active fundraising for the university. Most of the other women principals acknowledged that raising outside funds for their colleges was a necessity; however, one recently appointed principal expected to be able to continue in her previous role as an active scholar.

An experienced Cambridge principal stated that she was pleased that her college fellows had recently voted unanimously, after long discussion, to accept a gift of £4.25 million which she had personally initiated and which would enable them to build a new block of student residences.

Despite the need to fundraise, the major portion of the energies of the Oxbridge heads of colleges goes into academic programming. In contrast, the presidents of private colleges and universities in the United States candidly admit that the majority of their time is spent in activities that are directly or indirectly related to cultivating potential donors and acquiring gifts from private individuals, foundations, government sources, businesses and industrial firms.

Career preparation and professional development opportunities

While most principals felt that their previous experiences in academic committee work, civil service, or diplomatic assignments served as relevant background for the demands of their present positions, many expressed an interest in professional development programmes. None was aware of any British programme for men or women presently holding or aspiring to senior positions in higher education administration. The situation is quite different in the United States.

In *Investing in Higher Education: A Handbook of Leadership Development* (1991), Madeleine Green and Sharon McDade, former Director of the Harvard Institute for Educational Management, state that, 'In the past it may have been possible for presidents to get by as role models, good intuitive managers, and seat-of-the-pants leaders. But the complexity of the presidential job today makes it more difficult.' They quote George B. Vaughan (1986) who has studied the exits of community college presidents as a means of investigating the topics of presidential preparedness and effectiveness. Vaughan has found that presidents who leave their positions early are most often those who lack the 'organizational skills required today; they make costly blunders that would be avoidable if they had the necessary skills.' Green and McDade address the question, 'Given the position's demands and the lack of formal preparation, how can a president acquire the skills and abilities needed to lead in today's complex environment?'

Vaughan (1986) argues that the position of president of an American college and university 'is often viewed as the culmination point of a career that has been years in the making.' However, the path leading to the presidency is not now as straightforward as it was in the past. Green and McDade observe that, 'Where presidents once typically followed a predictable progression to their post, their backgrounds now vary increasingly, ensuring that each brings a unique set of experiences to the presidency.'

Conclusion

In comparison to the professional experiences of their US counterparts, the range of backgrounds and interests of the British women interviewed was marked. They frequently moved into higher education as proven leaders who had been highly successful in another sphere.

The appointment of the Head of the Victoria and Albert Museum as Vice-Chancellor of the University of East Anglia is an example. Perhaps it should be noted that a particular quality exhibited by this group is flexibility. Their skills may vary, but they all are willing to learn new ones, particularly those necessary for fundraising. Their lives are generally stable, often with husband and usually with strong family relationships. They enjoy their jobs, and on the whole have learned to cope with stress. Once established in their posts they are seen as capable managers and leaders of their institutions.

I find the versatility, adaptability and leadership ability of this remarkable group of women, as well as their intelligence, integrity and goodwill, heartening. The American Council on Education's 1993 Women Presidents' Summit envisioned its participants from around the world joining forces to develop a new global agenda for peace and prosperity. The Summit affirmed that such an image of connectedness 'is conceptually, visually, intellectually, and bodily associated with life-giving force, a power philosophically and historically relegated to the private realm of women.'

Bibliography

American Council on Education (ACE) (1993) *Overview of the 1993 summit.* Washington, DC, ACE.

Green, M. F. and Atwell, R. H. (1993) 'A view from the United States: forces for change'. *Policy Perspectives,* 5(1) Section B, June.

Green, M. F. and McDade, S. A. (1991) *Investing in Higher Education: A Handbook of Leadership Development.* New York, American Council on Education/Macmillan.

Griffiths, S. (1991a) 'Britain backward on sex bias'. *The Times Higher Educational Supplement,* 5 October.

Griffiths, S. (1991b) 'Right note with women.' *The Times Higher Educational Supplement,* 27 December, p. 4.

Higher Education & National Affairs (1992) 'More women leading higher ed institutions'. 41(11), 1, 3, 8 June.

Hodges, L. (1992) 'Women's circuitous routes to the top'. *The Times Higher Educational Supplement,* 18 September.

MacGregor, K. (1990) 'Outlook bleak for female factor.' *The Times Higher Educational Supplement,* 7 December, p. 4.

Ozga, J. (1993) *Women in Educational Management.* Buckingham, Open University Press.

Perry, P. (1992) 'Prospects poor for women.' *The Times Higher Educational Supplement,* 6 November.

Touchton, J. G. and Davis, L. (1991) *Fact Book on Women on Higher Education.* New York, American Council on Education/Macmillan.

Touchton, J. G., Shavlik, D. L. and Davis, L. (1991) 'Leadership at the top: women presidents in public, four-year institutions' in J. A. Sturnick, J. E. Milley and C. A. Tisinger. *Women at the Helm: Pathfinding Presidents at State Colleges and Universities.* Washington, DC, American Association of State Colleges and Universities.

Touchton, J. G., Shavlik, D. L. and Davis, L. (1993) *Women in Presidencies: A Descriptive Study of Women College and University Presidents.* Washington, DC, American Council on Education.

Utley, A. (1991a) 'Women profess to salary bias.' *The Times Higher Educational Supplement,* 30 August, p. 6.

Utley, A. (1991b) 'Women lose out on jobs.' *The Times Higher Educational Supplement,* 27 December, p. 1.

Vaughan, G. B. (1986) *The Community College Presidency.* New York, American Council on Education/Macmillan.

Part 3

Implementing Change

8

Through the Glass Ceiling: Networking by Women Managers in Higher Education

Christine King

It is a commonly-held belief amongst both men and women who are active in promoting the careers of women that to achieve any recognition women have to be better than most of their male peers. Higher education is no exception. Many women are outstanding in their achievements and are willing and able to take on the top jobs, but the number who are given such an opportunity is small. Whilst women are making advances into senior positions, albeit slowly, quite evidently the senior academic and managerial positions within the old and the new universities are currently still predominantly a male preserve. There are women who are beginning to wonder if the struggle to get there, and to bring en route all their different skills and talents to the workplace, is really worth the effort, and there are others who feel themselves quite definitely struggling against a backlash.

Demography and the crisis of British management, economy and, some would argue, society, together make women's contribution to a range of professions, in a wide variety of roles, not just desirable, but essential. Within the world of the universities and colleges, where so many institutional mission statements include an open commitment to equal opportunities, the slowness of the progress of women to the top is both apparent and, at first glance, surprising. Women are entering the profession at junior levels, are researching, publishing and teaching and are declaring themselves ready to take on managerial or leadership roles. It is clear that many women have the range of skills and talents needed not only to succeed but to bring a fresh dimension to a profession undergoing rapid changes and facing tremendous challenges. When will the number of women professors and vice-chancellors reflect this growing body of talent and innovation?

It might seem, now that we have equal opportunities legislation, we simply have to be patient and wait for women to 'come through'. Women, however, do not start at the same place on the career ladder as their male peers. By upbringing and by the attitudes which men and some women have towards them in their climb upwards, and by their own experiences en route, women get discouraged and positively impeded in their progress. We know that women constitute half the workforce in the UK and we see that they earn, on average, only 75 per cent of the salaries of their male counterparts. We know that less than 3 per cent are in top management jobs across the public and private sectors and that the situation is not visibly improving. We can count the number of women vice-chancellors and heads of institutions on the fingers of two hands and the block on women entering the professoriate is currently a matter of media attention.

Change clearly will not come in a gentle evolutionary way and women have ceased to wait for this, with many leaving the profession and others giving up on ambitions to reach the top. Without significant numbers of women at the top to act as role models, to begin to penetrate the myths and rituals and to start to decode what can often be the esoteric language and behaviour found there, few women will be able to break through their 'glass ceiling' and some of those who do will simply flounder.

There is an argument that says that women simply have to 'learn the rules' and that until they do, they will not succeed. Such an argument would suggest that women and men have the same kinds and varieties of skills and styles of leadership and management, and that any 'positive action' is not only unnecessary but wrong. Some women do, indeed, appear to lead and manage in a way which could be described as 'male' but they are few and the exception. For these women, who start with a style which emulates the existing male norms, there is a need to win at the men's own games. This is difficult because women, through their upbringing if nothing else, are often different to men in the ways in which they relate to others and consequently in the ways in which they manage. Thus to survive they have to learn new games and a new language, and to be unremitting in their practice of these. The world of education has in the past seen some strong women within this conventional model, and it is apparent from many of their biographies that their working lives constituted a continual struggle to be accepted. The uniqueness of women in such positions of prominence made them both isolated and visible. For many the loneliness and a feeling of being a stranger in a strange land were the costs of their success.

Increasingly, both men and women are identifying those characteristics of a 'female' style of leadership which women can bring to top jobs. Just as for the early pioneers who had to develop a syncretism of their own style within the unchallenged practices and assumptions of their day, so those women who have the courage and confidence to challenge existing norms and make changes need support and role models. Any woman who has sat as the sole or one of the few women at a departmental meeting or an academic board will know that the position can be one of great tension and discomfort. One woman alone at the meeting will be an oddity and her views idiosyncratic, two or more, and the situation improves dramatically.

Thus women who are in, or moving into, positions of power need to network. Whatever the encouragement they receive from their male colleagues and however much they are anxious not to be seen to be 'different' from the men, the open discussion and support gained within a formal or informal women's professional network is invaluable. Networks offer a 'safe place' for women to explore their own style and solutions, they operate as an information system and they provide contact with women who are both accessible and role models. These women do not have to be in complete harmony; they certainly do not have to be card-carrying feminists.

Setting up a network

At the end of the 1980s, a group of us who were newly appointed to positions of leadership within the then polytechnics and colleges sector within the UK came together to formalize and extend to others the support network we were starting to develop between ourselves. We were heads of department and deans, some were professors; all of us were conscious of being fairly unique in our own institutions. We shared the fact that we faced new challenges daily, in new jobs and in a rapidly changing sector. We were aware, although not in any campaigning sense, that our solutions, separately developed in each of our own situations, were often very different in content and style from those being operated around us by our male colleagues. We were aware of doors closed to us and, indeed, closed to at least some of the men we worked with, and we were conscious of the need to articulate and share some of the thoughts and experiences which we, as women managers, were having.

From this starting point the network 'Through the Glass Ceiling' was created, with its formal launch in January 1990. Some 40 women managers in higher education were invited to the offices of KPMG Peat Marwick McClintock in Birmingham to discover whether there was a need to establish such a network. The conference was largely conceived and organized by Dr Diana Green, now Pro-Vice-Chancellor of the University of Central England in Birmingham. Diana and I snatched time to plan the event and met more than once in a motorway coffee shop half-way between our two institutions to formalize arrangements. Had we waited for more appropriate times or meeting places, the event would never have happened. The conference decided overwhelmingly that a need for a network of senior women managers did exist and most of those 40 women became the founder members of the organization. Since then many more have joined and the network is flourishing. The meetings on the motorway became the first of a number of planning and administration sessions where a small group, with the help and involvement of our highly supportive secretaries, managed to make time in overloaded lives to set up events and organize ourselves professionally. The fact that we found that time is a measure of the group's commitment and also of the real importance for our working lives which the network came to assume.

We started with the proposition that women do offer styles of management and leadership that are often quite different to those demonstrated by most men in such positions, although we recognized that not everyone would agree. John Adair's book, *Great Leaders* (1989), has one of his 15 chapters dedicated to women as leaders. He tells of warrior queens, of leadership in marriage and of Margaret Thatcher. We learn that Adair sees no special characteristics of women leaders and reassures us that, if the market place fails us, we can still achieve leadership as wives, mothers, neighbours and citizens. Such reinforcing of stereotypes encourages women who fail to reach the top to blame themselves for not belonging or 'getting it right' and there is no recognition of the possibility that women will redefine some of the norms. There are ways in which, not always deliberately, women side-step many of the male totems of hierarchy and ignore what are traditionally seen as the trappings which constitute power and status. Women leaders are often more informal, are good team leaders and know how to get the best out of their people. Women managers often liberate staff and ideas and are unconstrained by rules and taboos because they are outsiders to this particular male language. What we aimed to do in 'Through the Glass Ceiling' was to identify issues of management and leadership style and culture as, in our experience, these related to women, and to explore ways in which these might be developed within our own profession and institutions.

The 'Glass Ceiling' manifesto identifies the issues:

> Increasingly, although slowly, women are entering the upper echelons of management in higher education. They move into a predominantly male world and many find themselves operating in a radically different culture, with different perceptions and assumptions, excluded from all sorts of male networks. It can be argued that women can, and do, bring clear and different skills to management, as well as the more traditionally professional skills. These 'female' characteristics, which may be, for example, about delegation, working in teams, sharing credit, high social and interpersonal skills, are shared by some men and are highly regarded in some management systems, but can be undervalued in the traditional British male management and institutional culture.

The choice of the 'glass ceiling' theme for our group represented some of the key issues for women within the management of higher education. The glass ceiling, a barrier which prevents women from rising, whilst real enough from below is often invisible from above. Men at the top can look down and ask why women are not achieving and, seeing no barrier, can only surmise a lack of talent, commitment or energy. Identifying just what that glass ceiling consists of, finding ways to break through it and ways to persuade those in power that they could help in this process became an important aim for the network.

The single most important way of achieving these aims was, we felt, to encourage women to network. Networking could help those who want to rise to positions of leadership, could encourage women to work towards a senior post and could offer support to the pioneers who are already at the top and may still be picking from their bodies the shards of glass ceiling which clung as they came through. Indeed, networking, we felt, may well be the single most important tool in women's advancement in the 1990s. Networking offers guidance, role modelling, support and a translation and courier service as women take their steps to the top. It accords well with women's styles of working which use communication and team-building skills to a significant degree.

Networking in practice

Far from being an artificial device, women at all levels appear to find the process stimulating and empowering. Sharing skills and information is something women outside professional life have long tended to do. Only the barriers of hierarchy and competition dominant within the world of management have encouraged women to see power as something to be retained rather than shared. Women in all kinds of situations network; young mothers meet and share information about child-rearing, for example, just as the traditional women's organizations, like the Women's Institutes, provide a focus for shared interests. The nature of networks is such that they work best for those who share current concerns and experiences. As the children grow so the mother moves into a different network and her role in relation to new mothers is one of advice rather than networking. It might be argued that women's socialization makes them good, on the whole, at making contacts and sharing vital information with their female peers, quickly establishing a common bond and communicating in an open way. This is in contrast to the well-developed mythology about all women being in competition over men and acting destructively towards each other. Women can act in this way, and when they do so it is often a reflection of their lack of voice or power elsewhere. As the women's movement has opened up for women the possibility of the support and friendship of other women, so the myth has been demonstrated to be just that. It has been part of the role of the networking movement to encourage women to challenge accepted ways of behaving and relating to others as they reach the top of their profession and to work with their strengths.

Professional networking is primarily about women in similar fields or on similar career paths meeting to make and share contacts. Members of the network, whether it is formal or informal, are likely to have common experiences and aspirations; most importantly, they share information and advice. In spite of the declared traditions of democracy and the new culture of managerial 'communication', women in higher education, at all levels, as teachers, administrators or managers, continue to be excluded from many sources of information and thus this aspect of networking is particularly valuable. At the level of senior management, there are normally so few women working within a university or college that whilst they will know each other, their scarcity makes any overt cooperation both apparent and subject to suspicion. In a meeting where there are five women and 40 men, if five men gather at the end of the meeting to compare notes nothing is seen as amiss, but if the five women sit together or gather together after the meeting the fear of plots or jokes about shopping and gossip can be heard from all quarters. Networking takes this contact into a wider arena where women meeting to talk with a common agenda outside of their own institution and with professional colleagues from other places is both more acceptable and safer. Thus women will meet to exchange news and ideas and may well have systems to ensure support for women colleagues and a welcome induction for new arrivals.

It was the need not only to find other female colleagues, but to share experiences across the sector which fuelled the growth of 'Through the Glass Ceiling' and the many other networks for women in higher education. 'Glass Ceiling' now spans the old and new universities and colleges of higher education as well as the academic and administrative worlds. Out of a meeting at an international conference for women in Vienna came contact between senior colleagues in higher education and the further education sector, and the FE women managers network was founded.

A common ground of interest together with a spread across different institutions offers a very powerful support system. It is often easier to discuss a problem in confidence with a colleague outside of the organization and the fears aroused in-house are less than if the network contains only the women within that college or university. Even wider networks, it must be said, do arouse fears and the suspicion that women are offering and demanding unfair favours of each other, at the cost of men. If it is accepted that many, although clearly not all, men do have access to ways of communicating and impressing their male bosses and have strategies for 'getting on', such objections to women networking are hard to justify. The fear that women in networks operate at a level of favouritism which is both inappropriate and damaging to their institution is generally unfounded. Good networks lay the ground rules very carefully, and the kind of relationships which women within them have preclude unprofessional requests or collusion and outlaw any exploitation.

Women's networks do not work like secret societies; they simply replicate, in a manner appropriate to their members, the kind of mutual support and shared language which men take for granted. If this appears more intimate than exchanges between men then this is a result of how women tend to communicate. The 'old boys' network', from which the new movement in networking takes its name, traditionally operates on debts of loyalty and seeks to ensure the promotion of its own. At the highest level, members share a public school or Oxbridge background and operate a cabal, rather than a support and information system, which seeks to empower its members and to allow them to achieve to their highest potential. A good women's network thus provides a range of contacts who, within a context of trust and mutual respect, offer immediately the kind of access to information and practical advice which it might take a woman many years to develop, and from which many women remain excluded all their lives.

The rules, which in formal networks are best clearly articulated, hinge around confidentiality and sensitivity. A woman in a position of management or leadership is in a difficult position in relation to other women, both in her organization and outside of it. She can be seen to be granting unprofessional favours if she has a special relationship with women who are junior to her, and the resentment which follows can harm her, her female colleagues and any aspirant women lower down the system. Since the rules of promotion and patronage stem from the traditional male culture of the business world, women at all levels are unsure of the unwritten rules and uncertain about the dividing line between making themselves visible and not asking for special favours. Networking can give these relationships a context and a framework and allow women to offer support and advice both up and down, with clear guidelines. Networks provide a safe and workable framework for mentoring, work-shadowing and other schemes designed to allow women access to the language and practices of a range of work experiences.

The advantages of networking are many. Women see other women in positions at their own or higher levels and the visibility of women's success is immensely encouraging. The pleasure women get from seeing that they are not the lone star they felt they were is observable. Some networks commission specific training, others operate a skills exchange. In either case members are free to identify, without appearing 'weak', those areas where they need help. At the same time, they know that in other topics they can share their experience and knowledge. Such an exchange is empowering and in a daily work context where, whatever management training manuals advocate, it is still less than acceptable to acknowledge ignorance, it can be immensely liberating.

One of the features of women's networks which can be misinterpreted is the amount of laughter which accompanies meetings. It is easy to stereotype this as women being frivolous, but in fact it serves a vital function. In a work situation, male and female laughter can have very different meaning and the laughter is often about very different things. Since laughter is bonding, a sole woman in a team of men may feel obliged to join in their humour for all sorts of reasons, even when she is not comfortable with its content and tone. With other women, the opportunity to use laughter to express shared feelings is very healing.

Some networks actively monitor the progress of their members and of women in their organizations, in others this is done by means of simply exchanging news. All networks, especially those for more senior women, operate informally as a platform for opportunity. Through sharing information, women learn of jobs and of opportunities about to come up. Recommendations can be made, references given and head-hunting take place. To many successful men, all this would seem unremarkable and the stuff of their daily professional and social life, but for many women it is an eye-opening and new experience. Women are, on the whole, simply not in the frame when appointments are made to committees, ad hoc working groups and public appointments. Unless they take some action to help themselves, it is doubtful if more than a handful ever will be and clearly this is a waste since a large number of women, already in middle and senior management posts, demonstrably have the ability to offer a great deal which is professional, creative and valuable. A lot of informal mentoring goes on within networks and some operate more formal systems. Members provide a source of information about well qualified and able women to those seeking to offer opportunities to women.

Women who are new to senior positions and who appear different to interview panels can be dismissed as a threat or simply as not 'being ready' for a senior position since they do not demonstrate knowledge of 'the rules'. If they express ideas which appear to be so challenging that they can be dismissed as naive, then their exclusion can be argued to be justified. Here again, networks can help women articulate a language and style which is both individual and allows them to communicate with the existing culture. Hopefully, through discussion, example and support, groups can help each other maintain their individuality enough to make significant changes, where these are needed, when they reach a position of leadership. Helping women get onto the path to the top, stay on it without collapsing from loneliness or isolation and still maintain their own ways of working is a major role for any successful professional network.

Is there any argument for including men in such networks? Clearly the principle of women-only groups raises fears not only in men but also in women who are anxious, for personal and professional reasons, not to be seen to be associated with something 'feminist'. Herein lies a dilemma. The 'safe' environment, which early women's groups identified in women-only meetings, is a necessary prerequisite for some networking activities. There may well be occasions when men are invited as speakers or guests, but it is important that the initiative lies with the women. Particularly interesting is the relationship with 'new men' within the world of education, who have a political or genuine commitment to equal opportunities and women's issues. Women need and value their support and mentoring and will find that men truly committed to women's advancement will not try to appropriate women's issues as their own.

It could be argued that the contacts women need are not those of women but of successful men and, given the realities of power structures within higher education, clearly there is an important role for the male mentor. This is undoubtedly true and most mentor schemes use both men and women as mentors. This is only part of the story, however, for women need to develop their own rather than their mentor's style. Where there are few role models and where the norms are, inevitably, male, the danger for women is that they will learn ways of managing which are alien to them. Not only will they not necessarily be very effective in this strange land, but they will cease to effect the kind of challenges and changes which the public and private sectors so desperately need. Confidence, numbers and a chance to explore within a safe but honestly critical context are, it could be argued, vital for the kind of success women need to reach the top, not just in ones and twos but in significant numbers. There are male and female managers within higher education who are doing a great deal to encourage this long march of women. There needs to be a cohort of women ready and able to take the opportunities created and to create, in turn, opportunities for others. One way in which this process can happen is through networking. 'Through the Glass Ceiling' flourishes, as we celebrate the successes of members and welcome newcomers. We meet for training and for information-sharing sessions and throughout we continue to build our networks.

Widening the network

Throughout we have been aware of other areas where networking might assist women in the educational world. We were conscious of the need to encourage and support women moving from their first or second post in the system into positions of more responsibility. Many of these were not yet at the level of seniority which we had defined as appropriate for membership of 'Glass Ceiling'. We were aware also of the need to network outside of higher education, with women from other parts of the educational sector and from other public and private industries. Many members of 'Glass Ceiling' developed strategies, formal or informal, of taking these issues on. Within my own institution, Staffordshire University, we have developed the Professional Women's Development Network which attempts to encompass some of these needs. Part of the work of the group, which is funded by the University, is with women who work for the University, in any capacity. Thus, for example, a mentoring scheme has been set up involving women mentees and men and women mentors, together with a series of other activities. The Professional Women's Development Network also runs a network for women managers in the region and about 80 members, from education, the health service and a number of private industries, meet on the last Wednesday of each month. In our management and professional development plans for women we have included our local further education and school partners so that the network grows ever wider. We are learning that one way to get through the glass ceiling, which all of us believe to exist, is to push outwards the glass walls in which we work by increasing our knowledge of and contact with women in different fields. We all have a great deal to learn from and share with each other. Clearly the future will look different for women within higher education and the networking which goes on will have a lot to do with achieving that goal.

Bibliography

Adair, J. (1989) *Great Leaders*. Guildford, Talbot Adair Press, pp. 245–69.

King, C. E. with Atkinson, M., Robinson, A. and West-Burnham, J. (1993) *Breaking the Glass Ceiling: Effective Management Development for Women*. London, Hodder and Stoughton.

Segerman-Peck, L. M. (1991) *Networking and Mentoring, A Woman's Guide.* London, Judy Piatkus Ltd, p. 17.

FE Senior Women's Network, details available from Ann Limb, Director, Milton Keynes College.

The Professional Women's Development Network, details available from Maureen Atkinson, Head of the Professional Women's Development Network, Staffordshire University.

Through the Glass Ceiling Manifesto, details available through Jeanne Caesar, TGC Administrator, 9 Cloverfield, Welwyn Garden City, Herts AL7 1EG.

9

Work Shadowing: A Positive Management Experience?

Ruth Gee

A shadow, as the name implies, is someone who follows another person about all day as he [sic] goes about his normal work. In this way, a genuine, inward understanding of that work is obtained by the shadow, which could not be obtained by a simple briefing or organised visit. Ideally, the shadow should spend an uninterrupted week or fortnight with his opposite number, but if that is impracticable, a regular visit of one day a week throughout the term would be satisfactory.

(David Lodge, *Nice Work*, 1988)

Much of David Lodge's writing has been set in the world of higher education and although it tends towards a parody of academia, it seemed an appropriate way in which to open this chapter, especially in the absence of any serious research into the subject. His definition is an appropriate one, stressing as it does the naturalness of the experience; the fact that it is important for the person who is being shadowed to do the things he or she normally does, to avoid the creation of an artificial environment which can happen on visits or briefings.

It is also important not to view work shadowing as a pale replica of work experience, which is much more readily recognized and indeed is now widely practised as part of the statutory and non-statutory educational experience. Work experience involves the individual in actually doing the work, practising the art of skill application before needing to be able to do so in a genuine economic environment. In planning for work experience, the student will wish to identify objectives which include industry-specific knowledge and operational understanding as well as the broader key transferable skills now recognized as critical to successful working life.

Work shadowing focuses on the individual learner rather than the material to be learnt. It is a learning experience within natural surroundings where participants already have knowledge and the learning process is being developed.

David Kolb (1983) identified the Russian cognitive theorist L. S. Vygotsky as the first person to expound the theory that learning from experience is the process whereby human development occurs. He believes, however, that the educational value of experiential learning, which I would claim is what work shadowing is, has an underlying theoretical base in the work of Dewey, Lewin and Piaget. In 1958 Dewey wrote:

> The modern discovery of inner experience of a realm of purely personal events that are always at the individual's command and that are at his exclusively as well as inexpensively for refuge, consolidation and thrill, is also a great and liberating discovery. It implies a new worth and sense of dignity in human individuality, a sense that an individual is not merely a property of nature, set in place according to a scheme independent of him . . . but that he adds something that he makes a contribution.

In his turn, Kurt Lewin developed the concept that learning is best facilitated in an environment where there is dialectic tension and conflict between immediate concrete experience and analytical detachment; whereas Piaget's theory was that intelligence is not an innate internal characteristic of the individual but arises as a product of the interaction between the person and his or her environment. For Piaget, action is the key.

It is taken almost as axiomatic in modern society that learning is a lifelong process; that the demands and needs of the economy, the changing work patterns and impact of technology all require this to be the case in the interests of the nation and that it is no longer a personal luxury of self-indulgence. In fact the future learning society represents a real challenge for millions of adults for whom learning should now be a central lifelong task essential for personal development and career success.

The writing of this chapter arose from that challenge and from a personal vision and experience which I wanted to share. In seeking to give the personal vision and experience a more learned and academic framework, I set about researching the topic, only to find very little writing about work shadowing amongst executive peers generally and nothing about further or higher education exclusively. Inevitably therefore, what follows is a personal record and a statement of conviction which, as yet, has no research base.

Further and higher education is big business; universities and colleges individually manage multi-million pound budgets and the sectors together literally billions of pounds of public money. Although they are factories for ideas, and academic and vocational qualifications, they require the rubric of the modern commercial company if they are to succeed within the post-16 market place. Their human resource development (HRD) programmes ought to be comprehensive and coherent and their budget allocations substantial. I believe that work shadowing schemes ought to be integral parts of those HRD programmes and that they are an excellent tool for personal management development, especially for women. These convictions come from my own experience as both shadow and shadowed whilst in chief executive positions in further and higher education.

Personal experience of shadowing

I acknowledge that a great deal of my success at a middle/senior management level was due to the positive role model I had in my boss. Although the polytechnic I worked in had no formal scheme for mentoring, I received a lot of help from the man at the top who took an interest in the progress of my career. He expressed his confidence in my ability and performance in a way which developed my own self-confidence and helped me to think the unthinkable for my personal career boundaries. The process, however, was informal and there was no structured mentoring scheme, which has its practice rooted in a similar educational theory to that of work shadowing. When I became the chief executive of a college of higher education, I acknowledged his role and determined to seek not only to develop myself further, but also to try to offer more formal opportunities to others and in particular women who are so woefully under-represented in the top jobs in universities and colleges.

My first work shadowing experience was to shadow the vice-chancellor of a traditional university. My recent career had been in public sector higher education and I wanted to understand more fully and assimilate the culture of the other side of the binary line (now abolished by government legislation). I wanted to be exposed to alternative practice, in particular about decision-making, staff contracts and rewards and governance.

Once I had decided what I wanted to do, the first thing was to get the agreement of a sympathetic vice-chancellor. The principle of agreement proved relatively easy, the practice of determining dates and discussing logistics less so. This has been my experience in all shadowing arrangements subsequently so it does not reflect adversely on the vice-chancellor involved. I think it is rather that the participating executive (referred to hereafter as the shadowed) tends to assume that he must have a work schedule which looks coherent, yet controllable. As we know, management is not a neat and tidy activity which can be readily arranged into discrete time slots. It is a complex activity, shaped by the micro-political and cultural context in which it is taking place. It involves dealing with the unexpected and the unusual, the mundane and the extraordinary. It is therefore essential that, once the shadow and the shadowed have agreed to participate in principle, they fix up the dates, preferably for a continuous week (I shall return to this issue) and be prepared to stick with them whatever the temptations to change.

As close as three days before my shadowing was scheduled to take place, the vice-chancellor's office phoned to try and rearrange it; shadowing would need to involve an overnight visit to London, which included a breakfast meeting with the chair of the board in his club and a royal reception. Far from putting me off, the prospect enthralled me! I have been eternally grateful to the vice-chancellor involved for agreeing to proceed. The scheme did involve me in shadowing him through a number of other more mundane events and the variety of his working week was a lesson in itself. But the lesson and principle to be applied, I believe, is the need to ensure that you are able to shadow a genuine working week and not to seek to manipulate its contents.

The university experience allowed me to assimilate and understand the culture more comprehensively and usefully than I could envisage from any other method. In addition, it helped me to understand the universal management maxim that there are no magic formulas for success, that all good practitioners are not only capable of making mistakes but do so and survive! I believe that my philosophical objective of keep cool, keep calm and keep on going stemmed from that time. I accepted, perhaps for the first time, that the world is not usually shattered as a result of any actions you might take and that there is more to be gained if you relax and enjoy the process of management.

That work shadowing experience convinced me of the value of making it an annual personal development event, and that I have sought to do with some success. The acquisition of alternative cultural knowledge and an insight into an alternative 'inside track' have each year proved invaluable to my learning experience and personal and professional development.

I have also been the person shadowed. It is perhaps worth describing that experience in some detail, too, as it was determined through a positive desire for women to be mutually supportive. My shadow was a female assistant director of a college of further and higher education. When she and I discussed her objectives, which I believe ought to be another early stage of the arrangement, she said that she wished to observe another management style and that of a woman holding a position to which she might aspire, as her next possible career move. She wanted to use the time to try to enhance her self-confidence and also use it as a period for reflection on her practice and that of her own institution. I agreed because I wanted to support another woman's aspirations for career enhancement. I realized it would also give me the opportunity to reflect on my own practice – a rare commodity.

Benefits of shadowing

Experience as both shadow and shadowed leads me to recommend the practice of work shadowing as an integrated and formal part of an organization's HRD programme. I do so for a number of reasons. Work shadowing is inexpensive, and in an era where cost-efficiency is essential and likely to become even more so, this is no mean consideration. There are no real costs for the person shadowed as she or he is continuing with their usual activities. For the shadow there will be the cost of time not spent on other activities, but I would argue that the personal investment costs will be more than offset later. There may also be some accommodation and travel costs.

It provides a non-threatening learning experience in an alternative work place. This can be particularly important for women as they find themselves as part of a small minority at the top. Although I experienced some teasing about *Nice Work* and the sexual innuendo thereby implied, it was not excessive, was very good humoured and non-threatening. Indeed the work shadowing experiences always provided an entrée into unfamiliar environments with the support of a third party, whereas in the everyday practice of being a female chief executive you often have to enter and deal with them alone. This way is far less daunting! Another great attraction and benefit I would suggest is that work shadowing not only introduces you to an alternative executive environment but it helps to dispel the mystique which so often surrounds it. When I shadowed the senior partner of a major accountancy firm and advised him of this fact, he was both amused and perturbed; part of the power position lies in maintaining that mystique and using it in your relationship with other organizations. Once you discover you can understand a world which hitherto has been shrouded in professional mystery and which you assumed was beyond your ken, you enjoy an enormous fillip to your personal self-confidence. Women are often led to believe that if their training has not been in finance and resource management they should not occupy top managerial positions. This is becoming increasingly true in education as colleges and universities are responsible for large budgets and men seek to protect themselves against the advance of women, whose formal education and training is still generally more artistically biased.

Work shadowing also offers the opportunity to reflect on best management practice. It is important to build in the time at the end of the week to reflect on the shadow's thoughts and observations. I have usually found that it becomes a part of a daily discussion but you should not leave it to chance and should structure it into the programme on at least one occasion. There is great value too in the couple meeting about three months after the experience. What learning do you remember at that stage? Has it impacted on your work activity in either a direct or indirect way? This monitoring and review process can be indispensable.

You may acquire some hard new knowledge and skills as a result of the exercise, but it is the formal and informal information, too, which can add so much to your personal portfolio. Learning how others manage their time is a valuable lesson and you may come away with some practical tips. It is interesting to observe the differences and similarities of approach to the same issue. Is private sector and public sector practice so different? Is not the aim of common purpose enhanced as a result of activities like this?

I believe, also, that work shadowing helps you to value the necessity of time out of the office. It helps to break the feeling, that is an increasing pressure, than one needs to deal with the in-tray and complete the tangible tasks. In essence, it values personal staff development and provides a low-cost creditable alternative to external courses and more standard forms of human resource development.

Implementing work shadowing

Every college and university in the country could introduce a programme of work shadowing for its senior staff team without too much trouble. I have found it relatively easy to use the annual appraisal interview to discuss development needs and identify a useful work shadow possibility. Once that is recorded in writing as part of the appraisal record, it is less likely to be lost in the pile of other good intentions. For some individuals I was able to rely on their own determination to pursue our agreement with little administrative assistance; for others more hand-holding and administrative support and direction were necessary. There are some basic ground rules to be observed.

Once the shadowed has been identified and the experience agreed in principle, the couple needs to establish if they have any particular aims and objectives. It can be helpful to set these down in writing. It is important to stress from the outset the confidentiality of the process. I have had more than one request turned down on the basis of concern about commercially sensitive information. I think it is less of a problem than people imagine but it is important to give some assurances and stick to them. I have found that it is not the information that you remember, but the process of management, the approach to problems and problem-solving. If you select a person to be shadowed who works some distance away from you, this is generally viewed as being less competitively threatening although this may be more a perception rather than a reality.

You hope that the organization has adopted work shadowing as part of a formal personnel policy, but the likelihood is that it has not, in which case you need to ensure that the chair of the board or equivalent is supportive, to avoid any potential subsequent backlash. It is also important for the person to be shadowed to notify his or her colleagues so that the shadow will not be embarrassed by awkward enquiries during the event. It is also helpful for the shadow to be sent any background reading in order to appreciate organizational structure and the like.

During the week in question, you will simply attend all the events with the chief executive and observe. People may be self-conscious at first, but that usually disappears quite quickly and you may even find yourself referred to or asked for an opinion. One of the positive spin-offs for the host organization is that you can obtain consultancy advice – free of charge! Ensure that the couple programme a time to debrief about the process both during the week and three months later. This can be done informally as well as formally. Indeed one of my most important lessons has been the realization that a lot of key strategic decisions are taken over the lunch table, or in the local wine bar.

The host organization may wish you to write a formal report, but I would discourage this as the essence of the experience should be the resulting personal development of the shadow. I have never been asked to write a report, but my oral debriefings have been described as invaluable.

Some large organizations such as the Civil Service and Leicester City

Council practice in-house shadowing schemes and organizations will vary the operational practice to suit their own needs, but the strength of my proposal, I believe, lies in the involvement of an external organization. While there has been a survey in the USA in 1986, I know of no British equivalent. The experience in the USA demonstrated that executive development is a key strategic tool and provides a competitive advantage. As a follow-up to the survey, James Bolt wrote in the *Training and Development Journal* in May 1990, that 'the foundation for new methods of executive education is being built on experiential learning.' In this article, 'How executives learn; the move from Glitz to Guts', Bolt identified four practical methods for executive education: outdoor experiences, business simulations, feedback, and customer involvement. Work shadowing might be seen as a practical manifestation of the latter two.

> The challenge to corporate education is to create new models for learning – models for developing new leaders, new organisational cultures, and new business skills necessary for competing in a global economy. Action learning is a direct out growth of such a bias toward action, and to using corporate education to change the organisation.

Although there has been no systematic adoption of work shadowing in higher education in the UK, Andrew Jack (1989) has written of the value of work shadowing in the David Lodge flavour, namely the exchange of information and practice between academics and industrialists, but his sample is very limited. There has been recognition of the value of a similar work shadowing approach for school students. In 1986, the DTI and IOD initiated a scheme in which sixth-form girls shadowed women executives. The subsequent Schools Curriculum and Industry Partnership (SCIP) encouraged a whole range of primary, secondary and tertiary sectors of the economy to allow themselves to be shadowed by school students and some college students. In his report of the scheme, Tony Watts (1986) drew some general conclusions which would be of value to both further and higher education in encouraging executive peer shadowing. The best practice came from those schools which had taken the initiative internally and had an institutional commitment to it; there is an excellent rationale for work shadowing in that it offers access to people and environment, feelings and emotions in a way which is economical in terms of time and pressure. He also highlighted the value of having some limited national support for the scheme.

Limited national financial support for a limited national framework for an executive peer work shadowing scheme would, I believe, be invaluable in realizing the leadership development which will provide the key to future success. David Kolb (1983) wrote that experiential learning theory offers:

> the theory for an approach to education and learning as a lifelong process that is soundly based in intellectual traditions of social psychology, philosophy and cognitive psychology. The experiential learning

model pursues a framework for examining and strengthening the critical linkages among education, work and personal development.

A systematic institutional and nation-wide approach to work shadowing could prove to be a successful practical manifestation of that theory for executives in higher education. Until that happens and systematic research is undertaken, it remains simply a personal conviction that work shadowing is a cost-effective and positive management experience.

Bibliography

Dewey, J. (1958) *Experience and Nature*, 2nd edn. Mineola, NY, Dover.
Jack, A. (1989) 'Workshadowing in Higher Education – what, why and where next?' *Industry and Higher Education*, 3, 4.
Kolb, D. A. (1983) *Experiential Learning: Experience on the Source of Learning and Development*. Hemel Hempstead, Prentice Hall.
Lodge, D. (1988) *Nice Work*. London, Secker & Warburg.
Watts, A. G. (1986) *Workshadowing*. York, Longman for the School Curriculum Development Committee.

Postscript: editor's note

Since this chapter was drafted the author has succeeded in attracting financial sponsorship for the introduction of a nation-wide work shadowing scheme for chief executives of colleges of further education. Forty work shadowing experiences have been successfully arranged and completed, to date. Individual chief executives from colleges have shadowed senior personnel in large private and public corporations. A research report on the findings of the scheme should be published during 1997.

10

Equal Opportunities Policy

Helen Brown

Introduction

The report of the Hansard Society Commission on *Women at the Top* commented (1990: 11), 'It is wholly unacceptable that the centres of modern academic teaching and excellence in Britain should remain bastions of male power and privilege.' Nevertheless the progress of women in HE continues to be painfully slow. However, on a more positive note, this issue is now being taken up by the Committee of Vice-Chancellors and Principals who published guidelines on equal opportunities in employment (CVCP, 1991) and subsequently established a Commission on University Career Opportunity which reported in June 1994 (CUCO, 1994). At a time when there is a new impetus to exploring and removing barriers to the advancement of women in both the public and private sectors, in the wake of the launch of Opportunity 2000,[1] it is timely to ask whether approaches to equal opportunities developed elsewhere can bring about much needed changes in the gender composition of the academy, particularly at senior levels.

In order to understand fully the 'demography' of the problem and to suggest possible ways forward we need to understand how the culture of HE acts to maintain the position of women as outsiders. Central to the dilemmas posed by the advocacy of equal opportunities practices are the current limitations of HE institutions as actively managed organizations (Brown and Sommerlad, 1992). In order to see how equal opportunities policies and practices can truly act to improve the status and representation of women we need to regard these as one example of management of change processes in higher education.

This chapter examines the current position of women in higher education and also draws on evidence from other parts of the public sector with a longer history of self-conscious equal opportunities policies. It suggests that the implementation of such policies may reasonably be considered as a necessary but not, in itself, sufficient condition to ensure that women are enabled to contribute fully to the world of higher education.

Table 10.1   Distribution of academic staff in new universities by gender and grade

FT academic staff 1991	Men (%)	Women (%)
Above principal lecturer	88.0	12.0
Principal lecturer	85.3	14.7
Senior lecturer	76.0	24.0
Lecturer	54.4	45.6
Total	76.2	23.8

The scale of the problem

A full assessment of the imbalances between women and men in higher education in terms of pay and position is hampered by the fact that there is less detailed information available about staff in the former polytechnic sector. The CUCO survey of 109 institutions in December 1993, while focusing on the extent of universities' equal opportunities policies and practices, also provides 1991 figures for the distribution of academic staff in new universities. These are reproduced in Table 10.1. The old universities are better served in that academic grade distributions are available for 1993, and two surveys carried out by the Association of University Teachers (AUT, 1991; 1992) provide some information on pay differentials. The situation will be remedied when the Higher Education Statistics Agency produces information relating to the whole sector.

Very recent figures suggest an improvement. It was reported in the Parliamentary debate of 7 March 1996 on equal opportunities that 50 per cent of university administrative staff are women, that 25 per cent are junior lecturers and that 5 per cent are professors. Even more recent figures compiled by the Higher Education Statistics Agency and supplied to the *THES* for the 26 July 1996 edition claimed that, by July 1995, 7.3 per cent of professors were women.

The figures for old universities (Table 10.2) show only a small increase from 1980/81 in the proportion of professors who are women (from 3 to 5.5 per cent) and recent figures, taken at best, show a further overall rise in the whole university sector to 7.3 per cent. Progress, but slow progress. Recent figures on lecturing staff also show some improvement to 30 per cent. However, there is also evidence (Aziz, 1990; Spurling, 1990) that women are disproportionately represented among those on short-term contracts – a form of employment which has grown rapidly in recent years.

Differences in average pay for full-time academic staff (1989–90) are shown in Table 10.3. Although these figures relate to 1990, they have not so far been superceded. The fact that women academics are overwhelmingly

Table 10.2   Distribution of academic staff in old universities by gender and grade

FT academic staff 1993	Men (%)	Women (%)
Professor	94.5	5.5
Senior lecturer	89.8	10.2
Lecturer B	79.8	20.2
Lecturer A	67.0	33.0
Total	84.1	15.9

Table 10.3   Pay differences for FT academic staff 1989–90

Grade	Men	Women	Men average salary (£)	Women average salary (£)	Women's pay as % of men's
Lecturer	20852 (64.4%)	5868 (87.6%)	17,310	15,985	92.3
Senior lecturer	7769 (11.6%)	699 (2.0%)	23,643	23,119	97.8
Professor	3782	133	29,228	28,069	96.0
Total	32394	6700	20,218	16,969	83.9

located within the lower points of the lecturer grade accounts for the overall pay differential of £3,249 between women and men. For the small group of women professors in the old university sector there is clear evidence of sex discrimination, with women earning on average £2,000 p.a. less than men (AUT, 1991).

This difference holds true for all cost centres where there are sufficient women in senior positions to make comparisons meaningful (i.e., excluding all sciences, where across all scientific and technological disciplines virtually all professors are men) and is regardless of age. The argument that women may reasonably earn less than men in similar positions due to being promoted later in their careers does not appear to be supported by these data, since the average age of women professors in the survey was the same as their male colleagues. In these circumstances we need to look elsewhere for explanations for these discrepancies. One potential factor is the way in which professorial pay is determined, and it is perhaps unsurprising that 93 per cent of women non-clinical professors surveyed supported a negotiated and published professorial salary scale, compared with 64 per cent of men. Senior women quite reasonably believe that informal and essentially secret mechanisms for determining the pay of individual professors act to their disadvantage, and that they would be better served by a system which is open and formalized.

Taken together these figures show clearly that the 19 per cent of full-time academic staff who are women are disproportionately located in lower grades and (where data are available) paid less than men in comparable positions through all grades. Perhaps of most concern is the lack of any evidence for a clear trend suggesting that the proportion of women as a whole, and in senior grades in particular, is increasing through 'natural' means. In the period between 1965 and 1994 the proportion of women undergraduates has increased from 28 to over 50 per cent, while the proportion of women in senior academic posts has increased to nothing like the same degree, falling well short of the proportion of women graduates in the age cohort who might now be reasonably expected to occupy senior positions. This strongly suggests that academe does not offer a welcoming or attractive employment option to many women. Women, it seems, are outsiders in the academic world.

One reason for this may be the fact that attention has not so far been given to understanding the issue in HE to anything like the same extent as in other parts of the public sector, notably in health and in central and local government. In the NHS, in particular, there has been a considerable volume of research over the last decade to identify the reasons for the under-representation of women at higher levels in the service and to identify possible processes of discrimination (Goss and Brown, 1991). Work within the NHS has culminated in the establishment of a Women's Unit within the NHS Management Executive and an energetic approach to instigating new enabling initiatives. These include the setting of targets for the proportion of women in different job grades, the provision of extensive development opportunities for women, and an insistence that good equal opportunities practice in appointments is adhered to. Targets have also been set by the Employment Services Agency. Within local government progress is more patchy; with some notable exceptions, most progress has been made in metropolitan authorities. It is worth noting, however, that the equal opportunities unit of the Local Government Management Board provides a similar central source of advice and support. In these parts of the public sector there are means which have been in place for some time to keep the issues of equal opportunities for women on the agenda of individual organizations.

Within higher education recognition that there is a problem which needs attention on a sector-wide basis (as opposed to the discrimination which individual women experience and understand) has come much more slowly. The guidance notes issued by CVCP in February 1991 were, at last, an acknowledgement that there may be structural factors which operate systematically to inhibit the appointment of women to a career in higher education and their subsequent career progression. These notes capture accepted good practice in equal opportunities and recommend *inter alia* public statements of equal opportunities policy, locating responsibility for its implementation with a senior officer of the university, equal opportunities training for those involved in recruitment, workforce monitoring and positive action. Relevant sections of this guidance are reproduced at Annex 1 to this chapter.

However, as Cottrell (1992) has noted, 'The guidelines were excellent on paper, but getting them off the page and into practice has proved difficult in most institutions and well nigh impossible in some.' In 1994 an optimistic view would be to see this as an over-statement of the situation. Ninety-three per cent of institutions which responded to the CUCO (1994) survey reported that they had formally adopted an equal opportunities policy. On the other hand, only 37 per cent have so far put in place action plans to implement their policies. This may mean that the gap between best and worst institutional practice will now start to widen.

Nevertheless there is no doubt that some universities are wholeheartedly and energetically seeking to implement active equal opportunities policies. The Hansard Society Report (1990: 10) cites the example of University College London where 9 per cent of its professors are women, compared with a national average of 3 per cent. The former Provost of UCL, James Lighthill, attributes this to 'a simple refusal to be linked by traditional preconceptions and misconceptions' (Spurling, 1990: 15). Leadership from the top is important, but it is also supported by very practical measures, including enhanced maternity leave and fully protected part-time posts which contribute to a situation where it is less difficult for parents to be working members of the college. Since the Hansard Society Report appeared, an increasing number of universities have signed up to Opportunity 2000, committing themselves to a programme of positive action and targets for the proportion of women in senior grades. The first of these, Sheffield Hallam University, now has an extensive equal opportunities programme and has recently succeeded in appointing a woman to an engineering chair. Their detailed and clear code of practice is prefaced by a statement from the Principal, John Stoddart, which rightly states that, 'Providing equality of opportunity is concerned with the elimination of discrimination by removing unfair structures, biased policies, prejudicial practices and oppressive behaviour.' Importantly, this statement recognizes that deeply-embedded features of organizational culture are likely to be major contributors to discrimination.

Another example of positive action comes from Sunderland University where, following the appointment of Anne Wright as Rector, an audit of the proportion of women in different grades and a series of equal opportunities training programmes for staff have led to increased numbers of women undergraduates and a higher proportion of women in senior staff grades. Again, similar elements of a successful approach are evident: clear leadership, accurate information about the composition of the workforce, and practical supportive measures.

Given the low level of women's participation in the academic workforce it should be relatively easy to make small gains, and it appears that those institutions which have taken positive steps have found this to be the case. However, it is much less easy to alter deep-seated cultural assumptions and we must be careful not to allow small gains to distract us from the bigger picture. The next section examines the main barriers to women's advancement.

Women's academic career – the barriers

The segregation of the labour force into 'women's work' and 'men's work' is well documented. This segregation applies to the top and bottom of an organization as well as to particular occupational areas. Consequently, women who wish to work in or advance in areas which are traditionally viewed as 'male' will have to overcome the barriers of convention and stereotypical expectations. This is no less true in higher education than it is in other areas of employment (see, for example, Thomas, 1990). Barriers of this kind are, perhaps, more subtle than, say, the demands of childcare, but they are undoubtedly real (Goss and Brown, 1991). For example, research into the realities of recruitment practices (Collinson *et al.*, 1990) shows that women are often judged informally and subjectively on the basis of their perceived 'suitability' for a post or for promotion. Judgements are made in terms of assumptions about commitment, ability to 'fit in', or about the assumed relevance of experience which may have little bearing on the post in question. Moreover, job-related criteria such as age are likely to be based on the career norms of the majority – that is, men – neglecting the fact that women are often older than men at the same stage in their careers. This form of discrimination was encapsulated in the 'New Blood' scheme, introduced in 1983, which was designed to encourage younger people into universities, which had an upper age limit of 35. Here a successful case was brought against the (then) UFC. The industrial tribunal ruled that the scheme constituted unlawful sex discrimination because the proportion of women who could comply with its terms was smaller than the proportion of men who could comply. However, the redesigned scheme for 'New Academic Appointments', while having no formal age limit, still enshrined the notion that academics are 'normally' at a certain stage in their career at a certain age.

These notions of 'suitability' and 'normal' career paths pose particular difficulties for women at all stages of their academic careers. In the early stages, Spurling's (1990) interview data with female and male Fellows at Cambridge graphically illustrates how men tended to drift into academic careers – it was simply a matter of going with the flow of their life so far – whereas for women there was a need to overcome positively lack of support or even active discouragement. Even before that stage women have generally learnt that they are less able, and tend to attribute their achievements to luck rather than capability. This self-perception is reinforced by a number of factors. For example, women get fewer firsts than men, *except* at the Open University where degrees are awarded essentially on the basis of continuous assessment; tutorials can often demand a confrontational, aggressive style which women are uncomfortable with; and they are far less likely to have women supervisors or tutors to provide role models. If women manage to get through that – perhaps by sitting at the back of the class and working diligently – when they move on to do research they have to fight their own corner, often without the support that men can, in many cases, take for granted. 'It's a knock-you-down, aggressive style' (Webster, 1992). It is striking that many reflections of women students and staff in higher education are a far cry from the situation of quiet contemplation and learning which outsiders may perceive. Instead they provide a picture of a highly political world, where success depends on ability to play the game by male rules. Assumptions of an environment based on collegiality and merit are more accurately seen as the consequence of 'illusion liberalism' (Thomas, 1990: 180) and a complacency based on the belief that the problem lies elsewhere as a result of gender stereotyping in schools, or the inadequacies of students. Failure to acknowledge the importance of either structural or attitudinal factors which limit the progress of women within HE institutions is a fundamental and deep-seated characteristic of academic culture.

Criteria of success

Ruth Deech, principal of St Anne's College Oxford and prime mover behind the development of the university crèche, is quoted (Goodkin, 1992) as saying:

> I have watched what goes on in libraries. The man will sit there from two o'clock and stay all afternoon. Maybe he'll rush off to college for a quick meal then carry on till late. The women will down tools at four, dash home, cook, wash up. By then she's too tired to do much. Without a publication record there is no promotion. Older women who have got their domestic problems out of the way then begin to publish. It is usually too late.

In spite of the fact that lip-service is paid to promotion criteria as a combination of excellence in teaching, administration and research, it is widely acknowledged that, in practice, promotion is largely determined by publication records. However, there is evidence that role expectations for female and male academics are different. Women are more often expected to play a major role in student support, by students as well as by faculty colleagues, in part because of inadequate performance in this role by many men, and in part because women students often prefer to discuss problems with female tutors. In the former West Germany, where the proportion of women in senior posts is similar to that in the UK, Hawkins and Schultz (1990) observe that while men are free to retreat into their own research without criticism, women are expected to nurture students, serve on committees, *and* conduct research.

The professional culture of academe relies heavily on networks, both as a means to and as a consequence of success. Essentially judgements about, for example, the allocation of research resources and the publication of articles and books are made by members of the academic establishment. What is presented ostensibly as a culture of peers and equals is more accurately seen as the operation of an 'old boy' network from which women may be excluded, or feel reluctant to intrude upon. In a review of research in the US, O'Leary and Mitchell (1990) found that research productivity is closely associated with the extent of an individual's networks and opportunities for collaboration. Women who characterized themselves as well-connected were more productive in terms of research outputs than low-connected women. Interestingly, 75 per cent of low-connected women described their particular interests as outside the mainstream of their discipline, suggesting that it is not only the volume of work which is at issue, but also the scope of what is perceived as proper academic work. This struggle can also be seen in the difficulties experienced in some institutions in the UK in gaining full support for women's studies courses.

Another study of differences in male and female research productivity (Davis and Astin, 1990) provides further evidence that women are subject to a greater range of demands on their time, both inside and outside the institution. They found that women, to a significantly greater extent than men, identified the time taken up by teaching, administration and their families as limitations on their research productivity. It seems clear that access to social networks, time and resources are critical factors which enable academic productivity; the absence of these factors creates barriers which often affect women disproportionately, and moreover do so at an early stage in their careers. Age, therefore plays an important role in productivity. Men reach their peak of productivity between 45 and 49, while women follow some five years later, between 50 and 54 (Lie, 1990: 112). Moreover, productivity and high academic rank in themselves act to attract research funding and thus lead to further productivity and enhanced reputation. As a consequence there are processes of cumulative advantage or disadvantage which reinforce early career positions.

Without careful consideration of whether these job norms are really job requirements, women, whose career patterns typically differ from those of men, will be placed at a disadvantage. There is a further twist to this wheel, as naturally women are aware of these factors, which in turn can lead us to adopt a certain caution in applying for new jobs or promotion. As outsiders women may well have different perceptions of what is important in the academic world and hence make choices about where to focus their time and energy which, in terms of achieving research productivity and reputation, are sub-optimal.

The other side of this coin is the fact that criteria for appraisal and promotion typically operate in a fragmented, piecemeal and inappropriately confidential manner. I am aware of institutions where the criteria for promotion are experienced as wholly opaque by the majority of staff. Although CVCP and AUT (AUT, 1992) have agreed joint recommendations on promotion procedures, there is still considerable variation between local practices. Most often promotions are made on the basis of recommendations of heads of department and thus have the potential to suffer from the exercise of local interests in the hands of (for the most part) under-trained managers. The myth of collegiality can obscure the many small exercises of discriminant behaviour which, taken as a whole, contribute to the clearly marginalized position of women in academe.

Equal opportunities approaches – strengths and limitations

The Hansard Society Commission recommended the appointment of equal opportunities advisers in all higher education institutions with responsibilities for monitoring and publishing the progress of women against targets.[2] The development of an organizational audit is an important first step in identifying where the women are. Equally important is the production of a dynamic picture which can identify how rates of career progression vary, linking these to training and other development opportunities. The initial audit should also consult with women and men to explore their perceptions of the most salient barriers to women's progression. In fact we already have substantial evidence about the main barriers. These include the following:

- women graduates are either not attracted to or fail to enter academe in comparison with male graduates. There are also suggestions that women drop out more often at an early stage in their careers;
- women find it harder to enter the supportive networks which provide access to mentoring and research opportunities;
- women's research productivity, particularly in the early years of their career, may be restricted by childcare demands;
- women tend to over-perform in the areas of teaching, student support and administration, to the detriment of their research activity;
- women are less likely to be appointed or promoted at all levels;
- academic careers are characterized by strongly held age norms.

Based on the particular diagnosis of a local situation, appropriate strategies for change may then be implemented. The Hansard Society Commission (1990) provides a useful checklist of strategies, grouped in relation to three main barriers to women – organizational, attitudinal and work and family. This list is reproduced at Annex 2 to this chapter. The implementation of all, or any, of these measures has the potential to improve the situation of women. However, there is no guarantee that they will do so unless the ways in which the organizational context within which they operate contributes to discriminant behaviour are understood and acknowledged. It is essential that whatever is done in the name of equal opportunities is central to an institution's mission and values, rather than a peripheral, marginal activity, only of interest to a few people within the personnel department. The instances of good practice which have been cited here perhaps also, and ironically, highlight the limitations of equal opportunities practices.

At their most fundamental, equal opportunities policies and practices provide the means for avoiding discrimination by ensuring that people are treated equally. This typically involves advertising jobs (rather than recruiting through networks), drawing up job and person specifications which can be justified, and ensuring that interviews and other selection processes are conducted in an unbiased way. It is unlawful to set job criteria which cannot be shown to be justified by the demands of the job, or which are more easily met by men than women. It is also unlawful to discriminate at the point of selection. Rigorously applied, these procedures are valuable, particularly in sparking discussion about the real requirements of the job. However, the test of equal opportunities procedures must be in terms of the outcomes – have they made any substantial difference to the proportion of women appointed or promoted? Whilst the appointment of a woman to a professorship or a directorate-level post is still rare enough to be a cause for celebration, the real challenge – the creation of an institution where this is not a rare event – often remains untouched. In local government, a sector with more than ten years' experience of equal opportunities policies, Coyle (1989) has concluded that little has been achieved. Some of the reasons she identifies for this failure can offer useful lessons for higher education as, hopefully, institutions respond to the encouragement to get policies 'off the paper and into practice.' The shortcomings of equal opportunities policies in local government include, at the most basic, an absence of a defined plan for implementation, monitoring or evaluation. More fundamentally, the assumption that 'fair' (that is, standardized and formal) systems for recruitment, promotion or performance appraisal can render gender stereotypes void, is seriously challenged. A number of commentators (see, for example, Jewson and Mason, 1986; Collinson *et al.*, 1990) have argued that, in practice, formalization of procedures is not likely, in itself, to make a significant impact on the representation in the workforce of any disadvantaged group. Realistically it is impossible to separate fully technical and functional job requirements from notions of 'acceptability' and 'suitability'. The danger is that narrow adherence to formal equal opportunities practices may make it appear that 'justice has been done' (Jewson and Mason, 1986: 55), while failing to address the informal processes of discrimination which continue to thrive. Moreover, the focus on individual achievement within a culture of liberalism and collegiality, which characterizes much of higher education, can effectively obscure or deny evidence of structured group disadvantage. In view of this, it is important that approaches to equal opportunities are not constrained to those which embody the same limitations.

A second dilemma is posed by the contradictory need to treat people equally but to attempt to compensate for past discrimination by treating people differently (Wilkinson, 1992). Such positive action usually depends on offering a range of training and development opportunities, both for those who are disadvantaged and for those in the privileged position. But higher education has a poor record in staff training and development. Whilst staff development has a key role to play in enabling institutions to deal confidently with the new challenges now facing them, the dominant model of staff development operating in universities is a fragmented and ad hoc approach, with the focus on individualized rather than organizational learning (Brown and Sommerlad, 1992: 183). Typically this means support for individuals to attend conferences or to take study leave. At present it is only in rare instances that we can identify coherent and self-conscious strategies for organizational development and institutional change. And yet these are essential if real changes in the level of women's participation in higher education are to take place. Without the development of some of the characteristics of a learning organization, based on collaborative inquiry, tolerance and questioning of the status quo, equal opportunities are destined to remain in a state of containment, salving the conscience of existing structures and relationships instead of transforming them.

One further specific problem that higher education will have to face if anything is to change is that of ensuring that academic life can be a viable and attractive career for women. Given the current low level of entry (and subsequent drop-out) it is by no means clear whether the next generation of senior women will be any more numerous than the present one. With few exceptions, people do not enter academe in mid-career and the pathway to the top is relatively narrowly prescribed, leaving little scope for unconventional careers.

Promotion is thus predominantly from within. The particular difficulty this poses is illustrated by the experience in BBC television (where there is a range of equal opportunity measures in place and a commitment to increasing the proportion of women in management posts). An internal survey (Equality, 1992) found that 50 per cent of those appointed from outside the BBC were women, but that women comprised only 21 per cent of those promoted internally to management grades. Where the pool of people who are eligible for promoted posts is confined to those who are already within the system, discrimination, as we have seen, is compounded at each step up the ladder. The need, although possibly not the urgency, to attract young women into academic life is recognized in the CVCP (1991) guidance notes. Quite how this is to be done or whose responsibility it is, is less clear.

Looking forward

The culture of higher education is highly resistant to change and yet change is occurring. Pressure to widen access and increase outputs runs alongside concerns about the financing of expansion and the implications for quality. Drives for greater efficiency and effectiveness are balanced by the requirements for more locally relevant provision and innovation in teaching and learning. These, and other factors, are making new demands on institutional managements which will require greater clarity and specification of organizational goals and the means of their achievement. This should not be taken as advocacy of 'managerialism' in a narrow, imposed sense, but rather that of creating a real sense of a collective organization complete with values and goals as a counterbalance to the traditional individual autonomy of academics.

There are a number of pressing reasons why it is no longer sufficient to view the under-representation of women in academic life as nobody's problem but their own. First, the recruitment and retention of women will be essential to the development of an energetic and effective higher education sector over the next decades. In 1988 women comprised nearly 40 per cent of those achieving postgraduate qualifications, and yet there is little sense that higher education institutions see themselves as competing with other employers for this valuable and expensive resource. A second important factor relates to diversity. There is now widespread acceptance in other areas of employment that diversity within teams (at all levels, including the very top) is to be valued over uniformity of experience and style, particularly where organizations are facing up to a rapidly changing environment. Limiting the 'models' of appropriate experience or the career pathways available to certain sorts of people can weaken the strategic thinking and problem-solving ability of an organisation (Goss and Brown, 1991). Strong leadership and managerial capacity depend on deliberately seeking diversity, and developing the capability to work with it. Third, most, if not all, higher education institutions are committed to widening access and equality of opportunity in education. But for higher education to develop in ways in which to meet these goals, it must also demonstrate that it can attract and develop a full range of staff in the same way. Finally, there are vital concerns of fairness and natural justice with which this chapter opened.

One final thought (for which I thank my colleague Sue Goss): *don't give up*. The current pressures for change which are permeating higher education may suggest that an agenda for equal opportunities is of marginal concern. Our experience of working with organizations is quite the opposite: once change has started, all sorts of things become possible; once traditional ways of thinking are successfully challenged, there are opportunities in all areas for radical ideas and innovation. Change is a good context for change.

Notes

1. Opportunity 2000 is a campaign promoted by Business in the Community which was launched by the Prime Minister in November 1991. Its aim is to increase the quality and quantity of women's participation in the workforce. Participating organizations are required to audit their workforce to establish the position of women, set targets and make a public commitment to these at the highest level.
2. Targets should not be confused with quotas, which are unlawful. Targets are best seen as reasonable goals which can be monitored over a given time period, such as recruiting a certain number of students or building so many miles of road.

Bibliography

Association of University Teachers (1991) *Pay at the Top of the University Ladder.* London, AUT.
Association of University Teachers (1992) *Sex Discrimination in Universities.* London, AUT.

Aziz, A. (1990) 'Women in UK universities: the road to casualization?' in S. S. Lie and V. E. O'Leary (eds) *Storming the Tower: Women and the Academic World*. London, Kogan Page.

Brown, H. and Sommerlad, E. (1992) 'Staff development in higher education – towards the learning organisation?' *Higher Education Quarterly*, 46(2), 174–90.

Collinson, D. L., Knights, D. and Collinson, M. (1990) *Managing to Discriminate*. London, Routledge.

Cottrell, P. (1992) 'Fairer university image'. *The Times Higher Educational Supplement*, 20 November, 4.

Commission on University Career Opportunity (1994) *A Report on Universities' Policies and Practices on Equal Opportunity in Employment*. London, CUCO.

Coyle, A. (1989) 'Limits of change: local government and equal opportunities for women'. *Public Administration*, 67, 39–50.

CVCP (1991) *Equal Opportunities in Employment in Universities*. London, CVCP.

Davis, D. E. and Astin, H. S. (1990) 'Life cycle, career patterns and gender stratification in academe: breaking myths and exposing truths' in S. S. Lie and V. E. O'Leary (eds) *Storming the Tower: Women and the Academic World*. London, Kogan Page.

Equality (1992) In house promotion of women: no change. London, BBC TV, 3: 1.

Goodkin, J. (1992) In a class of her own, *The Guardian*, 22 July, p. 19.

Goss, S. and Brown, H. (1991) *Equal Opportunities for Women in the NHS*. London, NHS Management Executive/Office for Public Management.

Hansard Society (1990) *Women at the Top*. London, The Hansard Society.

Hawkins, A. C. and Schultz, D. (1990) 'Women: the academic proletariat in West Germany and the Netherlands' in S. S. Lie and V. E. O'Leary (eds) *Storming the Tower: Women and the Academic World*. London, Kogan Page.

Jewson, N. and Mason, D. (1986) 'Modes of discrimination in the recruitment process: formalisation, fairness and efficiency'. *Sociology*, 20(1), 43–63.

Lie, S. S. (1990) 'The juggling act: work and family in Norway' in S. S. Lie and V. E. O'Leary (eds) *Storming the Tower: Women and the Academic World*. London, Kogan Page.

Lie, S. S. and O'Leary, V. E. (eds) (1990) *Storming the Tower: Women in the Academic World*. London, Kogan Page.

O'Leary, V. E. and Mitchell, J. M. (1990) 'Women connecting with women: networks and mentors' in S. S. Lie and V. E. O'Leary (eds) *Storming the Tower: Women in the Academic World*. London, Kogan Page.

Spurling, A. (1990) *Women in Higher Education*. Cambridge, King's College.

Thomas, K. (1990) *Gender and Subject in Higher Education*. Buckingham, SRHE/Open University Press.

Webster, W. (1992) Star Wars, *The Guardian*, 3 September, p. 32.

Wilkinson, B. (1992) Implementing equal opportunities. *Equal Opportunities Review*, 46, 25–30.

Annex 1

Equal Opportunities in Employment in Universities, CVCP Guidance, February 1991.

Summary of Recommended Guidance.

The CVCP's recommended guidance to each university is to:

- Reaffirm its charter by formulating and making known to all job applicants and employees a clear policy statement of equal opportunities.
- Formulate and make known to employees clear guidelines in implementing its equal opportunities policy statement.
- Consider, where appropriate, taking advantage of those sections of the Sex Discrimination Act 1975, the Sex Discrimination (Northern Ireland) Order 1976 and the Race Relations Act 1976 which allow for positive action.
- Assign overall responsibility for ensuring formulation, implementation, and monitoring of its equal opportunities policy to a senior officer of the university, such as the registrar/secretary.
- Identify from existing staff or appoint a suitably qualified and trained officer with a proportion of working time devoted to matters of equal opportunities in employment.
- Ensure that there is an appropriate consultative forum (or forums) with suitable membership including the trades unions in which matters of equal opportunities in employment can be considered.
- State on relevant recruitment material its position on equal opportunities in .employment.
- Issue guidelines on selection procedures setting out acceptable practice under the law and its equal opportunities policy.
- Ensure that so far as reasonably practical personnel staff, heads of departments and other employees who come into contact with job applicants are trained in equal opportunities.
- Give particular consideration to flexible working arrangements and schemes for those with domestic responsibilities.
- Keep under regular review the position of childcare facilities.
- Maintain a statistical record as comprehensive as possible.
- Report annually through its committee structure to its council or senate on the workings of its equal opportunities policy.
- Make efforts to reduce imbalances in the proportion of women employed at all levels in the university structure.

Section C: Employment of women in universities

1. The Committee is concerned at the imbalances in the proportion of women at all levels in the university structure for both full-time and part-time posts. It is especially concerned at the low proportion of women in senior posts in universities. The Committee *recommends* that efforts be made to reduce these and other imbalances.
2. A first step is for universities to identify whether women:
   (a) Do not apply for employment, promotion and training.
   (b) Are not recruited or promoted at all, or are appointed in significantly lower proportion than their rate of application.

(c) Are concentrated in particular types of contract (e.g. full/part-time, short term, etc.), grades, sections or departments.

3. This may be achieved by using information obtained from monitoring which will assist universities in:

(a) Comparing the proportion of women in specific grades within their institution against those in similar grades employed outside the university system.
(b) Comparing the proportion of promotions and regradings amongst men from one grade to the other with that of women in similar grades.
(c) Comparing the proportion of women in various academic grades with the relevant student intake.
(d) Identifying rates of application and shortlisting for women.

4. In the light of this data universities may then need to examine why particular trends exist and whether these can be justified. Reasons might include:

(a) Discriminatory selection or promotion procedures
(b) Time taken out of work for family responsibilities
(c) Inflexible working arrangements
(d) Lack of confidence and encouragement
(e) Absence of role models
(f) Institutional/individual attitudes
(g) Employer attitudes towards part-time working.

5. Where a university has identified areas of imbalance and possible reasons for these which cannot be justified positive measures aimed at bringing about change should be considered. These include:

(a) Agreeing a programme of action including setting up appropriate targets (as opposed to quotas which are illegal except for the registered disabled) and timetables against which the effectiveness of policies can be judged.
(b) Considering the 'positive action' provision of the legislation.
(c) Providing flexible working arrangements.
(d) Providing childcare facilities.
(e) Raising awareness of equal opportunities issues, particularly among those charged with selection, appraisal and promotion.
(f) As a long term strategy, encouraging women undergraduates and graduate students to consider a university career.

Annex 2

The Report of the Hansard Society Commission on Women at the Top, 1990.

Strategies for Change (adapted from Table 6.1)

Organisational barriers	
Unfair selection or promotion procedures	Equal opportunities policy
	Equal opportunities training
	Precise job specification
	Objective assessment criteria
	External advertising
	Equal opportunity audits
	Monitoring
	Targets
Inflexible working arrangements	Part-time/jobsharing
	Flexitime
	Working at home
	Other flexible arrangements
Mobility	Requirement dropped or modified
Age limits	Requirement dropped
Traditional roles	
Work and family life	Career break scheme
	Workplace nurseries
	Parental leave
	Enhanced maternity leave
	Other childcare help
Attitudinal barriers	
Lack of confidence	Equal opportunity advertising
	Encouragement to apply for posts
	Women-only training policies
Prejudice	Top level commitment to change
	Equal opportunities training

11

Reaching for Equal Opportunities: Models from Australia and the USA

Heather Eggins

Australia

Australia exhibits much innovation in its government's approach to universities but in certain respects the institutions themselves are still traditional. Although women make up 48 per cent of all university employees, they comprise only about a third of all academic appointments. Of those, only 18 per cent are at the level of senior lecturer or above. However, the situation has already improved markedly from 1986, when only 9 per cent of women were at senior lecturer level or above. The paucity of women at the most senior levels is still particularly marked at chief executive level, with the newspapers announcing proudly in July 1996 the appointment of Australia's third woman vice-chancellor.

Steps are already being taken which may help to change the attitudes of the community and appointing committees. Edith Cowan University, Perth, launched its Women in Leadership Project in 1992 with the prime objective of encouraging greater participation by women in the internal decision-making processes of the University. The project was developed by the Division of Human Resource Management and attracted widespread interest and support. It concentrated attention on the under-representation of women in senior positions but recently, in 1996, has been redirected to enhance the leadership skills of both men and women through a system of interactive workshops and mentor support.

The key feature of the project has been the development of a model which organizations of all kinds (higher education institutions, commercial and industrial companies and public sector bodies) can use to access the leadership potential of their staff by fostering organizational change and encouraging employees to become actively involved in the decision-making process.

A conceptual framework (Figure 11.1) has been developed which interprets the dimensions of leadership as bounded by the societal context and within that by the university context. Four different elements relating to an individual leader's capacities overlap with each other – those of being a

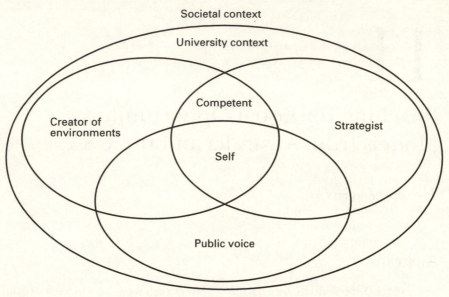

Figure 11.1   Conceptual framework
Reproduced with kind permission from Edith Cowan University, Perth.

strategist, being a creator of environments, those relating to work and identity, and those relating to the public sphere. The 'Framework of leadership capacities' is spelt out in much more detail in the following way:

Capacities relating to being a *strategist*:
Understanding the existing power structures
Having a clear vision of a desired future
Knowing the organization's procedures, policies and committees
Analysing the organizational culture
Recognizing potential allies and enemies
Understanding costing: personal, human, financial
Valuing risk taking, collegiality, patience
Making choices and decisions
Conflict resolution and negotiation
Managing discomfort and vulnerability
Knowing your limitations
Strategic planning
Debating skills
Communication skills
Cultivating mentors.

Capacities relating to *work and identity competence*:
Developing competence in scholarship, teaching and community service, research

Knowledge of industrial awards, organizational structures, funding struc-
tures, government policies
Understanding the impact of technology, political and academic changes
Understanding policies impacting on the institution, such as restructur-
ing, performance management, enterprise bargaining
Delegating
Facilitating.

Capacities relating to having a *public voice*:
Documenting achievements and views
Understanding the use of language
Making recommendations
Understanding media and mediums
Understanding the audience
Understanding when to speak and when to be silent
Using enquiry, putting views, negotiating
Representation: political, academic and organizational
Knowing appropriate forms of communication
Public speaking, debating and marketing skills
Valuing courage, sincerity, persistence
Capacity to summarize
Knowing your own image
Forming alliances.

Capacities relating to being a *creator of environments*:
Knowing the history of the organization
Shaping departmental structures and culture
Setting up a learning environment
Managing change, making a difference
Collaboration and cooperation
Valuing the capacity to take responsibility, the capacity to take risks
Maintaining personal, moral and ethical standards
Time management
Mobilizing resources
Team building
Valuing mutual respect.

The framework has, in effect, developed a new paradigm by which women's
contributions can be perceived in a new way. It draws on gender research,
change management theory and on theories relating to social movements.
It involves the willingness to be reflective, to value personal experience and
to make use of intuition. The framework is 'based on a sense of entitlement,
and a commitment to contributing to a workplace that is "owned" by all
workers, and to gaining recognition for real contributions that are being
made'. (Pyner, 1994: 5)
The view of those who developed the framework is that leadership is
concerned with four areas: behaviour that makes a real difference to the

operation of the institution in ways which support the interests of the institution, its staff and students; one's personal self in the workplace; 'connecting' the individual worker to the organization – for mutual benefit; and personal and ethical as well as positional rights and obligations.

The project has attracted more than 2,000 participants since its inception, drawn from a wide range of organizations. It has achieved international recognition for its innovative approach, proven results and contribution to the community. The activities are many and varied, including an annual public lecture series featuring prominent Australian or international women, an annual 'Women in leadership' conference, publications of its work and the conduct of research and training projects for public and private sector organizations. Its approach, which aims to link the role of individual staff with the future strategic development of the organization in which they work, has been shown to offer major benefits to both the individual and the institution, and can be perceived as a way of unlocking leadership potential within Australian higher education and society in general.

USA

The United States, as so often in educational matters, provides an example where the issues have been recognized earlier than elsewhere, and strategies have been put in place many years before others have considered what needed to be done. The problem posed by the handful of women chief executives of higher education institutions was recognized in the US by the early 1970s, a period when federal legislation relating to the cause of equal treatment for women in education was enacted. Examples of such legislation from that period included Executive Order 11246 which mandated affirmative action; Title VII of the Civil Rights Act of 1964 (as amended) which prohibited discrimination in employment on the basis of race, colour, religion, sex or national origin, and the Age Discrimination in Employment Act of 1967 (as amended), prohibiting discrimination on the basis of age.

The range of new laws were to act as a powerful means of bringing about new policies and new procedures relating to access to colleges and universities for students, and new opportunities for women and minorities in seeking career advancement within higher education. The social climate changed, making women leaders more acceptable within the community.

The part played by federal agencies at this period should not be underestimated. Apart from enforcing the equal opportunity laws, bodies such as the Fund for the Improvement of Post-Secondary Education, the Women's Educational Equity Act Program and the National Institute of Education funded projects in which data were collected relating to the status of women. Training programmes were devised and networks aimed at promoting women's advancement were initiated. Private philanthropic organizations also supported the change in the cultural perception of women, and both the Carnegie Corporation of New York and the Ford Foundation helped to

fund the establishment of a number of leadership development programmes. Thus women became increasingly more visible and society at large
began to appreciate more fully the value of women's potential contribution.

The provision of training opportunities for women who wished to achieve
high levels of leadership and administration within higher education was
widely perceived as essential. Some of the programmes begun in the early
1970s have, indeed, become an integral part of what is still available. One
which did not survive in its original form was the Institute for Administrative
Advancement established at the University of Michigan in 1973 to enlarge
the pool of 'qualified women leaders.' Its aim was to provide training in areas
such as budgets, legal issues, funding and institutional planning in order to
improve the effectiveness of administrators in colleges and universities. The
IAA evolved over time into a coeducational programme and ended its activities at the close of the decade.

A second group which became concerned with training was the Higher
Education Resource Service (HERS) begun in New England by a group of
senior women administrators. It began as a forum to discuss matters of
common interest and later established groups throughout the US and developed a number of training programmes to encourage and promote women
leaders. In 1976 the Summer Institute for Women in Higher Education
Administration was held at Bryn Mawr College, sponsored jointly by HERS-
Mid America and Bryn Mawr. This has been hugely successful, and has run
every summer since its inception. Other examples of the continuing work of
HERS is the West's group programme on institutional change and New
England's programme for administrative skills training.

Leadership training was also offered specifically to women in community
colleges, notably by the National Institute for Leadership Development
which grew out of a body established in 1973 by the American Association of
Community and Junior Colleges. The programme, named 'Leaders for the
'80s Project' began in 1981.

By far the most influential and wide-ranging programme, however, is that
offered under the auspices of the American Council on Education. This body
was founded as an independent, non-profit association in 1918 to represent
all accredited post-secondary institutions as well as national and regional
higher education associations. It 'coordinates the interests of all segments of
higher education into a single voice' and serves as the focus for discussion and
decision-making on higher education issues of national importance. Its functions are manifold, ranging from representing higher education before Congress, the federal government, the Supreme Court and the federal courts, to
conducting research and analysing data on American higher education. It
works with colleges and universities to improve the quality of higher education in numerous areas, administers the international high school equival-
ency testing programme, promotes understanding of issues concerning
international education and organizes the Business-Higher Education Forum.

In 1973 the Council established its Office of Women in Higher Education
which is advised by a Commission on Women in Higher Education composed

of member presidents of the ACE. The first focus for its activities was the enhancement of women's participation in higher education by helping colleges and universities interpret and implement a federal law which required equal treatment of the sexes in all educational institutions, as well as other equal opportunity laws and regulations. The Office still acts as a point of consultation on equity issues that affect women students, academic staff and administrators.

The second major activity of the Office concentrates on the advancement of women leaders in higher education, especially presidents of colleges and universities. In January 1977 a programme was created to identify, prepare and support deserving individual women for leadership roles, while at the same time encouraging the community to value women's leadership. It was named The National Identification Program for the Advancement of Women in Higher Education Administration (NIP). Substantial funding was provided by the Carnegie Corporation of New York, as well as money from the American Council on Education. Its major aim was to expand the pool of those qualified for leadership roles in US colleges and universities so that 'all women – black, Hispanic, Asian Pacific, Asian American, Native American and white' can have opportunities for advancement and so that higher education can benefit from their participation.

Its establishment followed on the findings of a Commission on Women in Higher Education set up by ACE in 1973. Their report, in 1975, showed that women accounted for 5 per cent of the chief executive positions. The total number of women heads of higher education institutions was 148, out of 2,500. Two-thirds were members of religious orders, and most of the others headed colleges primarily for women. Thus 132 of the 148 worked in private institutions.

The situation in the public sector was particularly acute, where only 11 women headed two-year colleges (the community college) and only five led four-year institutions, the mainstream universities and colleges of the US system. In commenting on the situation at that time, Shavlik and Touchton wrote

> the absence of women from positions of prominence did not mean that there were no women leaders in higher education, nor did it mean that higher education had failed to develop and use women leaders. The problem seemed to have been created by the relative invisibility of women as major leaders within and beyond their own campuses and communities.
>
> (Shavlik and Touchton, 1984: 48)

A telling paragraph from an article written in 1977, 'To advance women: a National Identification Program', by Emily Taylor and Donna Shavlik, reads:

> It is widely recognized that most jobs in higher education are filled by means of informal networks of faculty, administrators or other educational leaders who, by initiation or response, recommend promising

candidates for positions. Because educational institutions are largely male-dominated, so are the networks that spring from them. Even those persons who earnestly seek to advance women find themselves knowing few women to suggest for candidacy.

Donna Shavlik and Judy Touchton listed the barriers to women's achievements as they perceived them in 1984:

> These included a widespread belief within the higher education community that not many women were really qualified to assume major responsibilities within institutions, a lack of interest or an unconscious disinterest in recognizing and promoting women leaders, and a habitual inability to recruit and support women leaders. The natural tendency of executive management to select and promote people like themselves, the isolation of women administrators, and the tendency of women to compare themselves with an ideal of leadership (men compare themselves with other men) constitute other barriers.
>
> (Shavlik and Touchton, 1984: 49)

The way in which the National Identification Program, recently renamed the National Network for Women Leaders in Higher Education, is structured and delivered is thorough and impressive. Over 6,000 women and men give of their time and energy to help the programme succeed. It is delivered in each state, where the key role is that of state coordinator, usually a senior administrator, who is responsible for implementing the goals of the NIP.

State planning committees are then appointed, made up of representatives of all the higher education systems within the state. These are usually composed of 10–15 women administrators, numbering some 600 country-wide. Influential leaders of public policy within each state serve on state panels, in all about 750 men and women. They consider and devise what methods might best be used in identifying and advancing competent women.

At the national level, a panel of some 240 prominent academics is appointed to enhance the systems of state networks, and national ACE forums are held at regular intervals to provide a networking opportunity and exchange of ideas among women leaders and members of panels.

The range of work covered by the programme is extensive. Women executive seminars are held to enable groups of women with similar responsibilities to discuss issues of concern to them all. Distinguished women administrators near retirement are appointed as senior associates to the programme to share their knowledge and expertise with other women in the programme. Particular groups have their own special meetings to discuss their own issues such as that for women trustees. ACE/NIP regional forums give the opportunity to key people in the NIP to meet with others to discuss educational issues of regional concern and to extend their networks within each state.

The interconnections with other influential bodies are carefully planned. Formal links are set up with key national education associations to further the commitment of these associations to women's advancement. And finally, the NIP itself offers encouragement and makes nominations and recommendations of women well established in the programme for presidencies, vice-presidencies and deanships.

The work of the programme involves four elements. The first is the bringing together of people to let them 'catch fire,' so to speak, from meeting each other. The second is the use of 'consultative strategies.' Established leaders offer their help and advice in the planning and delivery of conferences, seminars and at smaller meetings, such as practice interviews and discussions of career plans. This is extremely valuable for the women in the programme and helps to increase their levels of confidence.

The third element is the use of 'systemic strategies' whereby the NIP is involved in the search and selection processes for administrative staff in general and, particularly, for chief executives. The Office of Women works with ACE's Senior Executive Leadership Service, a service to colleges and universities seeking help with identifying talented women and men for senior management positions. The service provides an additional link between the ACE Leadership development programmes (of which the NIP is one) and the institutions who might wish to employ the people emerging from the programmes. Linked to this is the ACE Roundtable of Executive Search Firms, created in 1985. Roundtable members, who are corporate members of ACE, are executive search consultants representing professional search firms, who work extensively with colleges and universities. The Washington Office of Women thus works directly with the search committees, presidents and board members to improve the search process, responding to requests for nominations, providing information about potential women candidates, and proffering advice regarding the search process.

> First, even before initiating a search, search committees and hiring authorities must openly address the issue of women in leadership roles so that unconscious or unexpressed bias against the hiring of women will not subvert the process. Second, the persons responsible for the search must be willing to stop the search process if it becomes clear that it is not yielding a candidate pool containing qualified women and minority candidates.
>
> (Shavlik and Touchton, 1984: 55)

Issues concerning the selection of chief executives are regularly discussed at national and regional forums. The ACE resolution passed in 1983 remains a touchstone: 'that presidents should be selected solely on the basis of their ability to carry out the responsibilities of the office.'

Finally, the importance of the individual developing new personal skills and capacities from the programme is stressed: 'The program works best for individuals who learn from it, and who work with the ideas that it presents.'

The effects of these various programmes are powerful in individual terms. Women gain a sense of worth and a recognition of their own abilities by having access to leadership positions in higher education and to those who influence leaders. Men develop new respect for women's leadership and an awareness that there are more women leaders than they ever imagined. The

Table 11.1 Number of women chief executive officers at institutions, branch and affiliate campuses, selected years: 1975–1995

Institutional type	1975 (31/12/75)	1984 (31/12/84)	1992 (15/4/92)	1995 (15/4/95)
Private	**132**	**182**	**184**	**237**
four-year	98	134	154	199
two-year	34	48	30	38
Public	**16**	**104**	**164**	**216**
four-year	5	32	58	78
two-year	11	72	106	138
Total women CEOs	**148**	**286**	**348**	**453**
Total number of institutions*	2,500	2,800	3,000	2,903
Percentage of women CEOs	5%	10%	12%	16%

* The number of total institutions used as a base from which to determine proportions of women and men in presidencies should be regarded as close estimates.
Reproduced with kind permission from the American Council on Education Office of Women in Higher Education.

community at large finds women leaders more acceptable and a more normal part of society. There has been little research undertaken on the effects of professional development programmes, and a direct relationship between programme participation and career movement has not been established. However, there are clear indicators of success in the numbers of women reaching higher positions. In the decade 1984–1994 the number of senior women administrators (presidents, vice-presidents and deans) has doubled. The figures for chief executives (presidents) are impressive. From a low base of 5 per cent in 1975, the percentage rose to 10 per cent in 1984, to 12 per cent in 1992 and to 16 per cent in 1995. The most recent figures show a total of 453 chief executives leading higher education institutions. Of these, 237 are private, with 199 leading four-year institutions, and 38 leading two-year institutions. The remarkable growth has been in the public sector, where from a base of 11 in 1975 there are now 138 in two-year community colleges, and from an even weaker base of five in 1975, there are now 78 leading four-year universities and colleges (see Table 11.1).

This represents a major achievement for the system. Some 20 per cent of current women presidents have emerged from the ACE/NIP National Forums, and of the more than 800 participants in the Bryn Mawr/HERS Summer Institute there have been many successful in gaining promotion and widening the scope of their work. Those who took part in the 'Leaders of the '80s' programme have similarly seen career advancement. There is no doubt that, taken together, the programmes form a very valuable set of networks which, linked to the executive search firms, provide a means whereby women's talents can be recognized and used.

Conclusion

Australia and the United States offer different responses to 'reaching for equal opportunities'. The UK could well learn from both. Indeed, it is ironic that of the 105 members of the Committee of Vice-Chancellors and Principals there are now six women, constituting 5.7 per cent of the membership – this is uncomfortably close to the US figure of 1975. The Commission on University Career Opportunity, established by the CVCP in 1993 for a period of five years to address issues of equal opportunity, contains in its objectives the intention 'to develop proposals for a national identification programme for the advancement of currently under-represented groups.' CUCO should certainly be encouraged, in its remaining time, to develop a model for the British system drawing on the lessons of the US. Likewise, it might well establish a pilot scheme to explore the efficacy of the Australian paradigm. Today's global communication systems enable the good practice of other continents to be recognized and learned from, to the advantage of all.

Bibliography

American Council on Education, Office of Women in Higher Education (1994) *A Blueprint for Leadership: How Women College and University Presidents Can Shape the Future.* Washington, DC, ACE.

Bensimon, E. M., Gade, M. L. and Kauffman, J. F. (1989) *On Assuming a College or University Presidency, Lessons and Advice from the Field.* Washington, DC, AAHE.

Green, M. F. (ed.) (1988) *Leaders for a New Era, Strategies for Higher Education.* New York, ACE/Macmillan.

Knopp, L. (1995) 'Women in higher education today: a mid-1990s profile'. *Research Briefs,* 6, 5.

Pearson, C. S., Shavlik, D. L. and Touchton, J. G. (eds) (1989) *Educating the Majority: Women Challenge Tradition in Higher Education.* New York, Macmillan.

Pyner, C. (1994) *Women in Leadership.* Churchlands, Edith Cowan University.

Shavlik, D. and Touchton, J. (1984) 'Toward a new era of leadership: The National Identification Program' in A. Tinsley, C. Secor and S. Kaplan (eds) *Women in Higher Education Administration.* San Francisco, CA, Jossey-Bass.

Sturnick, J. A., Milley, J. and Tisinger, C. A. (eds) (1991) *Women at the Helm: Pathfinding Presidents at State Colleges and Universities.* Washington, DC, American Association of State Colleges and Universities.

Taylor, E. and Shavlik, D. (1977) 'To Advance Women: A National Identification Program'. *Educational Record,* 58, 1.

Touchton, J. G. and Davis, L. (eds) (1991) *Fact Book on Women in Higher Education,* New York, ACE/Macmillan.

Touchton, J. G., Shavlik, D. and Davis, L. (1993) *Women in Presidencies: A Descriptive Study of Women College and University Presidents.* Washington, DC, American Council on Education.

Index

The Society for Research into Higher Education

The Society for Research into Higher Education exists to stimulate and coordinate research into all aspects of higher education. It aims to improve the quality of higher education through the encouragement of debate and publication on issues of policy, on the organization and management of higher education institutions, and on the curriculum and teaching methods.

The Society's income is derived from subscriptions, sales of its books and journals, conference fees and grants. It receives no subsidies, and is wholly independent. Its individual members include teachers, researchers, managers and students. Its corporate members are institutions of higher education, research institutes, professional, industrial and governmental bodies. Members are not only from the UK, but from elsewhere in Europe, from America, Canada and Australasia, and it regards its international work as among its most important activities.

Under the imprint *SRHE & Open University Press*, the Society is a specialist publisher of research, having over 70 titles in print. The Editorial Board of the Society's Imprint seeks authoritative research or study in the above fields. It offers competitive royalties, a highly recognizable format in both hardback and paperback and the world-wide reputation of the Open University Press.

The Society also publishes *Studies in Higher Education* (three times a year), which is mainly concerned with academic issues, *Higher Education Quarterly* (formerly *Universities Quarterly*), mainly concerned with policy issues, *Research into Higher Education Abstracts* (three times a year), and *SRHE News* (four times a year).

The society holds a major annual conference in December, jointly with an institution of higher education. In 1994 the topic was 'The Student Experience' at the University of York. In 1995 it was 'The Changing University' at Heriot-Watt University in Edinburgh and in 1996 'Working in Higher Education' at University of Wales Institute, Cardiff. The 1997 Annual Conference is entitled 'Beyond the First Degree' at the University of Warwick.

The Society's committees, study groups and networks are run by the members. The networks at present include:

Access
Eastern European
Funding
Mentoring

Vocational Qualifications
Postgraduate
Quality
Student Development

Benefits to members

Individual

Individual members receive

- *SRHE News*, the Society's publications list, conference details and other material included in mailings.
- Greatly reduced rates for *Studies in Higher Education* and *Higher Education Quarterly*.
- A 35 per cent discount on all SRHE & Open University Press publications.
- Free copies of the Precedings – commissioned papers on the theme of the Annual Conference.
- Free copies of *Research into Higher Education Abstracts*.
- Reduced rates for the annual conference.
- Extensive contacts and scope for facilitating initiatives.
- Free copies of the *Register of Members' Research Interests*.
- Membership of the Society's networks.

Corporate

Corporate members receive:

- Benefits of individual members, plus.
- Free copies of *Studies in Higher Education*.
- Unlimited copies of the Society's publications at reduced rates.
- Special rates for its members e.g. to the Annual Conference.
- The right to submit applications for the Society's research grants.
- The right to use the Society's facility for supplying statistical HESA data for purposes of research.

Membership details: SRHE, 3 Devonshire Street, London
W1N 2BA, UK. Tel: 0171 637 2766. Fax: 0171 637 2781.
email:srhe@mailbox.ulcc.ac.uk
World Wide Web: http://www.srhe.ac.uk./srhe/
Catalogue: SRHE & Open University Press, Celtic Court,
22 Ballmoor, Buckingham MK18 1XW. Tel: 01280 823388.
Fax: 01280 823233. email:enquiries@openup.co.uk

378.111 W872 1997

Women as leaders and
managers in higher